We, the Sovereign

T0087525

Gianpaolo Baiocchi

———————

We, the Sovereign

polity

First published in 2018 by Polity Press

Polity Press
65 Bridge Street
Cambridge CB2 1UR, UK

Polity Press
101 Station Landing
Suite 300
Medford, MA 02155, USA

ISBN-13: 978-1-5095-2135-7
ISBN-13: 978-1-5095-2136-4 (pb)

A catalogue record for this book is available from the British Library.

Library of Congress Cataloging-in-Publication Data

Names: Baiocchi, Gianpaolo, 1971- author.
Title: We, the sovereign / Gianpaolo Baiocchi.
Description: Cambridge, UK ; Medford, MA : Polity Press, 2018. | Includes
  bibliographical references and index.
Identifiers: LCCN 2018010020 (print) | LCCN 2018021112 (ebook) | ISBN
  9781509521395 (Epub) | ISBN 9781509521357 (hardback) | ISBN 9781509521364
  (pbk.)
Subjects: LCSH: Sovereignty. | Democracy. | Political participation.
Classification: LCC JC327 (ebook) | LCC JC327 .B2322018 (print) | DDC
  320.1/5--dc23
LC record available at https://lccn.loc.gov/2018010020

Typeset in 11 on 15 Sabon by Servis Filmsetting Ltd, Stockport, Cheshire
Printed and bound in Great Britain by Clays, Elcograf S.p.A.

For further information on Polity, visit our website: politybooks.com

Contents

Foreword

The book you have in your hands was completed in 2017, globally one of the darkest political periods in recent memory. It is hard to know if this moment will be one that will be remembered as having set us all on a path to even darker days of xenophobia, nuclear brinksmanship, and environmental fragility—or if this period will be remembered for having set us on another path, one charted by a generation of young people who, from Tahrir Square to Ferguson, from Avenida Paulista and Plaza Mayor, sought alternatives to representative democracy and market fundamentalism. The old, as the worn phrase goes, is dying but the new is not yet born.

Across the globe, and at the level of formal institutions, these are indeed very grim times. Whatever gains and optimism remained of post–WWII prosperity, of the 1968 social movements, and of Third

World independence struggles, seem to have entirely faded. We seem to be making very little progress on the global existential issues of our time, be it climate change, the global housing crisis, or world hunger. According to the *Bulletin of the Atomic Scientists*, we are closer than we have ever been to doomsday. At the same time, social scientists can barely wring their hands fast enough to keep up with the tidal wave of hard-right political sentiments across the Global South and North. Nationalist chauvinism in its various guises seems to have become an irresistibly resonant political lexicon. In Europe, fascist tendencies have found popular support and electoral footing throughout the continent, whether we are speaking of outright neo-Nazis or slightly more euphemistic versions that were part of the Brexit campaign.

Voters in Turkey and the Philippines have elected strongmen who seem to get more popular the more they flout basic democratic institutions. Meanwhile, the world's largest democracy, India, now has as its prime minister someone who was never fully cleared of his participation in ethnic pogroms and who stokes communalist tensions with nearly every address. And in Latin America, many of the so-called Pink Tide of left-of-center governments have fallen, some of them spectacularly, being replaced with a combination of market orthodoxy and social conservatism that harkens back to the dark years of the military juntas.

And in the United States, just as Black Lives Matter burst on to the scene, promising for some the dawn of a new civil rights era, a right-wing presidency has unleashed demons many people did not know even existed among the country's angry electorate.

The left is obviously in crisis in much of the world, unable, as of yet, to give a convincing response to this scenario. Social Democratic and Labor parties had been tilting right in an attempt to capture an electoral center, only to have their social base taken from them in many countries where right-wing movements have been better able to give expression, in however distorted a fashion, to discontent and existential fears. In response to the right's organizing and full-throated political talk of the "people" (however narrowly imagined), these parties have responded with arid (and pro-market) policies, in an odd way becoming defenders of an establishment that for so many has not worked. And leftist parties, here meaning the broad swath of political formations to the left of social democracy, have not fared much better. Reformed or rebranded communist parties in Europe have not managed much of an electoral foothold, while newer parties like Greece's Syriza have not managed to stay the course of a transformative political project. Most on the left recognize that we need to reorganize our institutional projects, but we have not quite figured out how, even if we should feel emboldened by the movements around us.

And the irony is that if leftism, as an institutional and political project, feels like it is floundering, it is *not* due to an absence of social mobilization or even the currency of leftist ideas. The early 2010s were marked by the Arab Spring, Occupy, Black Lives Matter, and movements like it around the world. The early 2000s were also a period of enthusiasm for the World Social Forum, which seemed to bring together anti-neoliberal movements from around the globe. It is almost as if there were two separate worlds: the vibrant world of movements and mobilization, and the sterile and uninspired world of political parties. The tragedy of the left today is that the former finds so little reflection in the latter. Finding our way back to that connection is, as I describe in this book, not only possible, but among our most urgent tasks.

One example among many is Bernie Sanders's insurgent candidacy in the Democratic Party primaries of 2016. Sanders, as is well known, is an independent senator from Vermont who self-describes as a democratic socialist. During the campaign, he was more critical of market orthodoxy than any major party politician in the United States in recent memory. He railed against the 1 percent, and spoke with admiration of some of the advances of Central American socialism and Cuban healthcare. Despite the fact that his campaign had little funding and was hastily put together, he garnered *millions* of votes among Democratic voters, in the end more than 40 percent of primary votes. This fact—that nearly half of registered voters of the Democratic Party offered their endorsement of a *socialist* candidate, has had very little impact on the party itself—which despite having been trounced by a far-right candidate shows no concrete indication of endorsing any more progressive economic or social policies or reforming its internal structure to become more democratic or open to grassroots inputs.

And while the US Democratic Party may be to the right of most social democratic parties, the example stands in well for the broader problem: the energies and democratizing impulses of social movements are currently disconnected from institutional politics. If it is in our movements, and in our life in common, that we invent, glimpse, discover, and prefigure the world that we want to inhabit, it is among institutions that we secure the conditions for that life to come into being. This book is about the connection between those two worlds and explores the theory of popular sovereignty, a leftist view of the link between democracy and rule.

Popular sovereignty is an emancipatory project. It is a radical reinvention of the idea of democracy, one in which a historic bloc of the oppressed makes up the center of a political community that is open, egalitarian, and democratic, and is sovereign over its own fate, fundamentally empowered to reclaim public grounds and institutions. It recognizes that in order for this egalitarian political community to fully emerge, state actions are necessary to continue to democratize society. And it also recognizes that existing state institutions are not structured for popular sovereignty and that they need to be transformed as they are enlisted, constantly held in check by both democratizing popular pressures imbricated in their midst and counterweights outside of its boundaries. This transformation is a political project that will encounter resistance from those used to benefiting from previous arrangements, so the popular politics activated by state reforms need to act as a counterweight to elite power. And implicit in its project is that its full realization transcends both nation-states and private property.

Foreword

Popular sovereignty, as a "piece on the checkerboard," does not often appear in the Anglo-American political lexicon, at least not on the left. The right, as with the Brexit vote, had no problem invoking the idea of parliamentary sovereignty in the name of a chauvinist project. In North America or in the UK calls for people's power often come from the right, the ideas entangled with nativism, racism, and fear of others. But the right's version of sovereignty is a closed political fiction, a parochial separateness that defines self-determination ultimately as the right to exclude others, a sort of turbo-charged NIMBY politics that protects hierarchies and private property. Yet even in the US and the UK there are other appeals to sovereignty that have a different valence: think of calls for indigenous sovereignty, Puerto Rican independence, or the Scottish independence movement. In each case it is a political logic that is generative, that is about *interdependence* more than about separateness, and that is quite compatible with egalitarian claims and anti-capitalist politics.

Popular sovereignty is a much more common concept on the left in Latin America and Southern Europe, where the idea of combining the energies and democratizing forces of social movements with strong state institutions in a mutually transformative relationship to advance social justice is commonplace and has many different inflections. Popular sovereignty finds expression in different ways in Barcelona en Comú; Podemos; the Workers' Party of Brazil in its heyday; the Bolivarian revolution; the Zapatistas; radical movements in Bolivia, Ecuador, and Uruguay; among many others.

The concept of sovereignty, if not the word, in fact, appears simultaneously and independently among nearly all leftist political formations on the Latin American continent in the 1990s. From Uruguay to Mexico and Puerto Rico, movements spoke in the language and terms of sovereignty, of self-rule, and of exerting that rule through state institutions. And nearly all spoke of exerting that rule nationally or even at a continental level. It is true that Latin America has a more "statist" political culture than, say, the United States, but national sovereignty had a specific and powerful valence on the left. It is beyond the scope of this book to explore why this might be, but in Latin America, the history of US empire and struggles against it is decisive. The history of independence and anti-imperialist movements loomed large over these movements, as did the more recent history of US meddling to undermine progressive regimes in the region. And the imposition of austerity measures only seemed a continuation of US imperial ambitions.

And it is important to remember, too, that those speaking of sovereignty are not old-style statist socialists. They emerged from the new, plural, rainbow formations of the era, who were looking very critically at Eastern European experiences as failures and quietly distancing themselves from Cuban Communist Party vanguardism, especially during its Special Period. In some cases, these activists saw the nation-state as a colonial artifact to be overcome.

The very concept of sovereignty in the Global North can have a much more negative association on the left; I know it is with this concept that I may worry some readers. For some, it is a concept too tied to ideas of the nation-state or to bourgeois ideas for it to be of any progressive value. For others, it is its decisionism that is the problem. Sovereignty implies closure, finality, borders, negation, the very opposite of the worlds that we are wanting to build. And some influential thinkers today make the argument that sovereignty means applying the general will to state institutions when that 'general will' is always partial and less than the 'will of all'—that sovereignty, in other words, risks cementing a partial view of the world. Others underline scale: some are comfortable with the concept applied to very local arenas, but much less so when we are speaking of higher levels.

The response to these qualms, and the reason the concept is valuable, is that there are too many pressing issues for us *not to act* on them through public action. As an example, the issues facing Latin American movements were myriad. Whether stopping the deforestation of the Amazon, reversing the privatization of natural resources, returning Maroon land to the original slave-descendant occupants, freezing bus prices, carrying out land reform, distributing school lunches, building housing cooperatives, expelling US troops, or reforming the police, each of these required state action that was sovereign, and unwavering, and beyond what social movements can do on their own. Many of the impediments holding us back from the world that we want are found in the form of state policies that need to be reversed or affirmatively deployed in order to make society more egalitarian. The key question is less whether or not to have sovereign action, but rather, *how to hold it in check through radically democratic means so that the state is a democratizing force*, creating openings and conditions for the social transformation that popular sovereignty implies, and not the opposite. It is not just any sovereignty that we want, it is a radically democratic people's sovereignty. It is not simply a matter of occupying the palace, or even of enacting socialist policies once there, but rather of continually transforming institutions—and ourselves—by making them subservient to the imperatives of a radically democratic and egalitarian community.

Very many of the important decisions in fact escape local, regional, or national jurisdictions. Indigenous communities throughout the Americas have demanded recognition, land rights, and the conditions for a dignified existence while demanding sovereignty. But if the first decisions to realize those aspirations need to be made by the national state, many subsequent ones have jurisdictions beyond the nation. Just as the "We" is open to constant reinvention, so is the concept of sovereignty, which can never be confined to national structures or thought about as some kind of isolated autarkic fantasy. As I briefly touch on in the final chapter of this book, global limit-cases, like climate change, force us to think about what popular sovereignty might mean in such overarching cases and what structures might support it.

Popular sovereignty is, of course, also political theory with a contradiction at its heart, at least in the radical democratic terms I lay out here. The democratizing impulse that formed the historic bloc that makes up the "We"—its openness, plurality, egalitarianism—is always going to be in some tension with the decisionism that sovereignty implies. So, when open, plural, and egalitarian movements have called for the people's sovereignty, they have done so fully aware that this would mean a set of engagements with potentially unpredictable outcomes. This is why there is a recurring stress on the importance of process throughout this book. The political project of popular sovereignty is not an end state. As I will insist throughout, it is always in a process of constant construction and reconstruction. It is ultimately impossible to answer the questions that popular sovereignty asks without imagining a radical transformation of society, one beyond private property and nation-states, even if the political project of popular sovereignty tells us less about that utopia than about the way to get there. And even then, it is more of a method than a road map.

And a word or two about me. I was eighteen when the Berlin Wall fell, living a bi-national life between Brazil, where I had been born, and the US, where I lived. I belong to the same generation of people that Thomas Piketty describes in the foreword to *Capital*—the first generation of adults to know only a world without the USSR and state socialism. I actually experienced the fall and its aftermath as a university student in Berkeley, California, one of the few places in the United States, I suspect, where the poignancy was so sharp. Many people were both elated by the images on the screen, but also sad. The images so clearly portrayed the very thing that activists value—the people taking charge of their own circumstances, pushing back against authority, making history. But this was also disorienting: it was not only that the Soviet Union was coming undone, or that unavoidable truths would now be coming to the surface. It was that the very idea of an alternative to liberal democracy and free markets seemed to vanish, nearly overnight. As terribly flawed as state socialism had been, it provided a counterpoint of some kind to the existing order. As with the neoliberal slogan, now there really seemed to be no alternatives . . . or at least no longer any assurances about alternatives.

My own return to Brazil in 1993 and subsequent work in Porto Alegre in the latter half of the 1990s put me in touch with a kind of leftist activism that had actually been freed by the fall of the Wall, now no longer fettered by the ossified imagination of bureaucratic socialism. I describe some of this in *Militants and Citizens*, a book based on my research at the time. A generation of activists—many, but not all, students—were shaped by their experiences in movements that helped usher in Brazil's transition to democracy from 1984–8, and then to successfully drive out a corrupt oligarch from the presidency in 1991. These activists, who drew inspiration from a heady mix of liberation theology, Paulo Freire, and Third World struggles, hardly glanced at Eastern European state social-isms, except as a negative example. It was they who re-invented unionism and movements for urban rights, by insisting on bottom-up democracy in spaces where popular voices were truly respected and in radical practices anchored in community solidarity. In a way that was novel, they combined radical democratic practices and an institutional leftist project of transforming institutions while engaging them.

At the same time, though, I also belong to a generation of activists in the Global North who have mostly lost political ground, and who have witnessed a global rightward tilt so sharp over our lifetimes as to be dizzying. Relatively common-sense social democratic ideas—market regulation, universal provision of healthcare and education—that in my childhood would have been a baseline from which leftists might push for equality and empowerment, are now fringe ideas of the far left. The college campus of the early 1990s was for a time a very exciting place from the point of view of activists. Many of us used to repeat the phrase that the 1990s would make the 1960s look like the 1950s. The Iraq War in 1991 only galvanized more students and protests, though in retrospect it returned Berkeley to what Berkeley does best, which is to protest war, which only postpones many inevitable questions. The election of a Democrat to the White House in 1992 drained a lot of urgency from activism, and the 1990s ended in an ambiguous way for activists. In one way, so many issues came to the fore for the first time during that decade; however, eight years of increasingly pro-market Democratic rule ushered in a new conservatism during the following Republican years.

As we turn to introspection and look for new ways of organizing, new ways of resisting, new ways to work with allies on short- and long-term issues, the same questions continue to surface. What should our relationship to institutions be? What about political parties? How do we scale up our politics? *We, the Sovereign* is meant as a contribution to this current, a short reflection based on a slightly different set of referents than the usual discussion in North America and the UK.

Foreword

Though the book draws on Latin American experiences, it is not meant to be a coherent analysis of all of these experiences, nor a compilation of the best practices from all of them. Rather, this is meant as a provocation to think differently about the possibilities for the left. And in doing so, I am revisiting the so-called Pink Tide in a slightly different way than many commentators. In Brazil, as for much of Latin America, the Pink Tide story is a contradictory one. Beginning in the early 2000s, left-of-center governments—originating in radically democratic social movements and unions—won national administrations throughout the continent, enacting policies that lifted millions out of poverty, that resisted US influence in the region, and that gave voice to dispossessed majorities for the first time in ways that would have been unimaginable previously in their respective societies. But, by and large, these governments often capitulated to powerful capitalist interests and seldom directly challenged their power; and too often, broader political structures remained unchanged and leftist political practices began to resemble those of the status quo. A decade later, many of these governments imploded, taking parties, movements, and aspirations with them.

But the Pink Tide is not Lula, or Evo, or Kirchner, or Chávez, or even Subcomandante Marcos/Galeano. It is also not the thousands of elected officials from leftist parties throughout the region, or even the good policies they devised in some places. It was a *tide*, and it began somewhere other than the national palace. The legacy rests with social movements and with countless mostly nameless activists who broke away from theoretical orthodoxies to develop new, and revolutionary, political practices in austere and repressive contexts. These practices, which *predated the national electoral victories*, centered on the arts of solidarity and coalition-making and engaging with institutions with the intent to transcend them. It is a tremendous disservice to forget these in the name of armchair inevitablism that reads the whole thing backwards from national-level disappointments. So it is these that I revisit.

This is an activist book. It is neither a cookbook of strategies nor a comprehensive program, but rather a book to think *with*. This book is a call for activists to expand our imaginations, an extended argument that our political projects may not be possible without a state and its institutions, and that engaging the state need not mean an inevitable road to technocracy or authoritarianism. But it is also written with the belief that it is a mistake for today's left to react to the populist right's rejection of elites and experts by retreating to technocracy, thinking that smart policies and ideas from above will carry the day. It thus seeks to force a return to the question of institutions by activists who have dispensed with them, and to democratize leftist thinking that has abandoned the energy of social movements in favor of institutional struggles. The position I advance here implies that we would not want to be part of a socialist project without the democratizing energies of social movements. It also means we would not want a political project that turned its back on the state either, as, in my view, it would then be vulnerable to involutionary powers or social pressures.

Its primary audience consists of the radical activists of the next generation, who, I am convinced, are not nearly as ideologically straitjacketed as the generations before them. Whatever their precise coordinates and orientation, whether socialist, autonomist, anti-racist, anti-facist, abolitionist, feminist, queer, ecological, or some combination of all of the above, this generation of activists is reinventing political practice in ways that are endlessly creative. As they lead us to our next politically transformative projects, it is important that they remember that this line of thinking and its consequences are part of their legacy, too. I have included as an appendix a small selection of excellent English-language books and articles for further reading that I think illuminate aspects of these experiences in greater depth than I can in this short manuscript.

Astute or scholarly readers will no doubt recognize echoes of debates with a number of authors. Paulo Freire, Ernesto Laclau, Antonio Gramsci, Enrique Dussel, Cornelius Castoriadis, Jacques Rancière, Cornel West, Nancy Fraser, Chantal Mouffe, Erik Olin Wright, Angela Davis, Marta Harnecker, Michael Hardt, among others, form a theoretical and scholarly backdrop for this book, but no more than that. It also draws from two decades of circulating in and near some of the worlds I describe and allude to, sometimes as a researcher, sometimes as an interlocutor, sometimes representing some of these experiences as an "expert," and sometimes as a participant. It also draws on informative discussions I have had in places ranging from Willimantic, CT, to Trivandrum in Kerala, among many others in between, where building popular sovereignty was on the table. And it has benefited tremendously from generous readings, particularly by *compas* from the next generation of activist scholars. Both the debts and disagreements should be obvious. But the debates need to be settled in practice anyway and it is to this purpose that I write. This book, like the politics that have inspired it, was always meant to be experienced without footnotes.

1

Movements and Questions
of Our Time

Radical politics are no longer the same. There is today a new generation of activists taking to streets and plazas demanding radical social change and actively imagining alternatives to the status quo. Some are demanding a complete transformation of institutions, wanting democracies that are meaningful and livelihoods that are less precarious.

For a brief moment in the early 2010s, the issue of democracy very dramatically and suddenly took center stage all around the world in the form of urban protests and occupations of prominent public plazas. In December of 2010, in Tunisia, protesters took to the streets and clashed with police following the self-immolation of Mohamed Bouazizi, a street vendor in the city of Sidi Bouzid. This very quickly reverberated all over that country (eventually causing the overthrow of the dictatorial regime), but also in neighboring countries. Over the next weeks, young people took to the streets and plazas demanding change in Egypt, Syria, Yemen, Libya, Morocco, and Oman, the so-called Arab Spring.

Partially inspired by this turn of events, Spain's Indignados next took center stage in that country the following March, while hundreds of thousands of people occupied the streets of Lisbon with the Desperate Generation movement. In Greece, the anti-austerity protests, which had been underway since 2010, intensified in May of 2011, with the Indignant Citizen Movement taking over public places all over the country. In Chile that same year, in August, students began massive national protests against inequality and cuts in education, in what some call the Chilean Winter. And in the United States, Occupy began in Zuccotti Park in September, before spreading to some 600 cities and towns across the country before the year's end and forever shaping a generation of young people who took part in it.

Just few months later, Brazil's June Protests of 2013 started as a protest against a 20-cent bus fare increase but became an inchoate set of protests on myriad issues in several different cities, bringing the country to a standstill for days. In July of 2013,

Movements and Questions

Patrisse Cullors, Opal Tometi, and Alicia Garza founded Black Lives Matter in the aftermath of the protests of the vigilante killing of seventeen-year-old Trayvon Martin. Black Lives Matter has become a loosely organized network with chapters and virtual chapters in many cities, and has decidedly changed the public conversation about police violence and racism in the United States. Shortly after that, Hong Kong's dramatic Umbrella Revolution of 2014 has made the issue of democracy on that island unavoidable. And as I write, national resistance to Donald Trump's regime in the United States, with networks such as #ItTakesRoots, seems to be changing the landscape of left politics.

This is only a very partial list of the most visible global protest movements and new radical politics arising in the last few years. A slightly longer list might also include Idle No More, the worldwide indigenous peoples' movement founded in 2012, the UK student protests of 2010, the Taiwanese Sunflower Student Movement of 2014, and many other anti-austerity protests throughout the globe. It might also include the Icelandic Pots and Pans Revolution of 2009, which led to the re-writing of the constitution, or the organizing behind Jeremy Corbyn's candidacy in the Labour Party in the UK, or Bernie Sanders in the US. And it might even include some of the energy around new political parties in Europe, such as Slovenia's ERP or Germany's Die Linke. And this doesn't even begin to mention local initiatives, including radical cooperatives such as Cooperation Jackson, in Mississippi.

Our Democracy / Their Democracy

Although the motivating issues are very diverse, there are some important commonalities that underwrite much of this recent organizing and many of these protests. Of course, the rejection of contemporary neoliberalism and the experience of precarity is a common denominator in many cases. There is also a strong undercurrent of claims for rights across these protests: the right to shelter, livelihood and existence, mobility, assembly, education, and healthcare is present across many contexts.

But most of all, there is also a strong uniting theme that representative democracy has failed to make good on its promises: it has failed to deliver meaningful representation, meaningful connection to a common condition, and a meaningful experience of control over the conditions of people's lives. Whether we are talking of World Cup megaprojects in Brazil, runaway police violence in the United States, or market fundamentalism in Portugal, in each and every case activists insist that the institutions of representative democracy do not allow regular people to make decisions concerning things that affect them. In each and every case there are elites (sometimes named, like "the 1 percent") making those decisions and benefiting from them. The institutions of democracy—political parties, elections, consultations—serve only as a buffer behind which powerful interests can hide, and limit people's imaginations by dictating what is sensible. Most of these movements prefigure—that is, they live out and model alternatives: defining features can be a commitment to horizontalism and sometimes leaderlessness, participatory democracy, and resisting traditional institutions. The archetypical picture that will remain in many people's memory of this period of struggle will not be barricades, strikes, or even mass protests—it will be the encampment, the temporary occupation, the *open assembly*: people sitting around in a circle discussing common concerns and platforms. And the open issue of "what next?" is one of the questions that faced nearly all of those participants.

A deep-seated suspicion of political parties, *including on the left*, is often an important corollary to these experiences. We on the left need to accept this fact as revealing of our failures, rather than with the paternalistic admonishment that was a surprisingly common reaction in many contexts. And activists across these settings no doubt have a clearer vision of what they do *not* want—authoritarian governments, neoliberalism and market fundamentalism, elite cities defined by displacement, police violence, gentrification, economic precariousness and poverty, and environmental degradation and injustice. What is much less clear across the board is a propositional vision—what might more truly, deeply democratic and egalitarian societies look like, for today and tomorrow?

This chapter introduces the main set of questions around democratic practice that these groups are grappling with, questions that are this book's primary concern. Everywhere these movements have been in tension with traditional representative democracy, and everywhere they have been inventing new practices. Yet there are also a number of questions these movements have been facing, such as the relationship to political parties and institutions, how central it is to have a programmatic platform, the relationship with other movements, and internal tensions around horizontalist principles. Nowhere has this been more poignant than with Spain's Indignados, and for this reason we momentarily turn to an international day of protest against austerity with an epicenter in Madrid.

15 October 2011

On this day tens of thousands of Madrileños—joined by many more Spaniards who had come in from far-flung corners of the country—flooded the city's downtown to converge at one of the city's historic plazas, the iconic Puerta del Sol. At this event marking the five-month anniversary of the original occupation of the Puerta, a broad swath of the city's residents—young and old, retired, working age, families with strollers—took their places in the six-hour march buoyed by the chants that the 15M movement, or the Indignados, had become known for: "if we can't dream, you won't sleep"; "they don't represent us"; and "these are our weapons" (as they lift their hands in the air, a sign of agreement at assemblies). The march culminated in an assembly, where thousands of participants sat down for a large group discussion, which then broke into smaller working-group discussions, every one

7

following the careful participatory methodology that had become one of the movement's signature features.

The Indignados were a complete novelty in an otherwise staid Spanish political system, and took many observers by surprise. The 15M evolved from a group that coalesced around an internet-based manifesto, the *Democracia Real Ya* (Real Democracy Now, shortened to DRY). The 15M (15 May) became the much larger and more diffuse movement that manifested itself that evening in Madrid. "They do not represent us," was one of its original slogans, as was "We are not goods in the hands of politicians and bankers." The original manifesto, which discussed unemployment, the mortgage crisis, and housing affordability, focused not so much on economics as on the breakdown of political accountability and representation. To some on the left, this focus on representation and political process was insufficiently radical, as was the movement's refusal to rally around specific platforms (which could only come after deliberative processes).

The original mobilization that gave the movement its name (15 May) was meant to coincide with the upcoming municipal elections of 22 May, and on that day, some 20,000 participants responded to DRY's call to show up at the Puerta. This was in part thanks to the support of some 500 organizations and movements, even though DRY rejected official collaboration with any political party or union or any other expression of "institutionalized political ideology." The success of the first event spoke to how salient the issue of citizen disaffection was in a moment of crisis.

What followed that first Sunday was not planned, and is today part of social movement lore in Spain. As the protest dwindled, a small group managed to stay overnight in the square. Twitter mobilization around a hashtag (#acampadasol), drew more people, and by the end of the week more than 10,000 were camping overnight at Puerta del Sol, with mirror occupations in Barcelona and Seville. 15M developed working groups on democratic procedures, financial transparency, mortgage reform, and a host of local issues. According to one survey, some *8 million* people say they participated in 15M events.

There was much that was novel about 15M: its central organizing principle of direct democracy, its commitment to respectful and open discourse, its transparency, and its constant reflection on questions of methods, such as deliberation and consensus. Newcomers were always welcome, and all were bound by the same rules, which forbade speaking of enemies, for example.

A corollary of the principle of direct democracy was the overt rejection of representation, bringing people together as equals. This was a shift from much social justice activism, particularly the logic of coalition-building. Spanish cities had for many years been with filled with networks and organizations focusing on very diverse interests: housing occupations, environmental movements, global solidarity networks, working-class organizations, anarchist groups, feminist collectives, among others. Until 15M, the work of advancing social justice consisted of suturing together often-fragile coalitions of representatives. Public decisions taken by 15M, on the other hand, were not based on a representation of any groups or specific interests or alignments. This caused tension with some social movement activists—rejection of a coalition logic and the focus on civility were viewed as potentially "reformist," which aroused suspicion.

But nothing was more controversial than the relationship to institutional politics. Hanging over the October march was the upcoming election. The movement drew on disaffection—its very slogans spoke of the incapacity of democratic institutions to represent everyday citizens, and of the way the political system benefited elites. At the same time, the issues that drew participants to assemblies in the first place—mortgages, unemployment, precarity and insecurity, the environment, public education— are ones that are fundamentally affected by policy choices that play out, for better or worse, in the political system. But to participate in the political system would mean for many to legitimate a broken set of institutions. The "useful vote" in this case would be to vote for the PSOE, an ossified and economically conservative Socialist Party. But to not participate would mean to give the right-wing Popular Party an assured victory. Their particularly neoliberal candidate was promising to roll back regulations on everything except for immigration, which he took an unusually hard line on. The decision of so many 15M participants to not vote, or vote blank, indeed delivered a decisive victory for the Popular Party. Coupled with the previous results of provincial and local elections, it put Spain under near-total right-wing dominance for the first time since its transition to democracy, and 15M was an undeniable part of that equation.

We, the Sovereign

From Indignation to Proposition

While the 15M movement reshaped the political debate in Spain, putting the question of disaffection at the center of the discussions, it did not provide answers to the questions it was able to raise. If institutions were broken, what sorts of institutions should replace them? If "they" do not represent "us," then who might? And how feasible, beyond a neighborhood movement or a very local issue, is it to run a democracy without *any* kind of representation? Can a movement really function without leaders? And what about politically conservative Spaniards—do they deserve a voice in a movement? And doesn't a movement of individuals—one that does not have set-asides or lobbies for underrepresented groups, say—risk simply reproducing social biases? What would the movement's relationship be to other movements, and to existing left parties?

Perhaps most pressing were questions about political representation—surely this movement ought to have a voice in Spain's institutions, but lots of questions remained as to what that might look like, and how to ensure that it would actually break with existing institutional patterns rather than be transformed by them. This was the subject of much discussion and debate among intellectual and political circles in Spain, a debate made much more poignant by the 2011 election results.

In January of 2014, a list of thirty activists and intellectuals presented a manifesto at an assembly at Madrid's Complutense University that would become the blueprint for a new political party. The manifesto, *Mover ficha: convertir la indignación en cambio político*, or "Make a Move: Turning Indignation into Political Change," sought to bring 15M innovations to the institutional arena. Key leaders from a variety of social movements, like the PAH (the movement of people affected by the mortgage crisis), and squatters' movements, as well as leaders of leftist formations, were present alongside some of the activists who had become prominent during the rise of Indignados. It combined abstract principles (the idea of hijacked democracy, the critique of representation) with some central demands: opposing austerity measures, keeping abortion legal, having Spain leave NATO, and prioritizing public interest over private property. After two days of debate and discussion, on 16 January a new political party, Podemos ("we can"), was founded and a new leader announced, the political scientist Pablo Iglesias.

The first goal was to compete in the next European Parliament elections in May: Podemos needed to garner 50,000 signatures. It did so within 24 hours. Within twenty days of allowing members to join, it officially became the third largest party in Spain. While its first run at the European Parliament was not entirely successful, it continued to grow. In the 2016 elections it earned over 20 percent of the popular vote, ending the two-party system in Spain.

While its success has been meteoric and its accomplishment profound, Podemos has not been without critics, particularly from social movement participants. A number of questions today circulate around it. What will prevent Podemos from becoming just another political party? What will prevent its charismatic leaders from ruling the party indefinitely? Now that it has quickly grown, what mechanisms are there to assure its internal democracy? Should it engage in electoral coalitions? Should local coalitions run independent campaigns at the local level? Is the party's insistence on a crisis of representation—seen as a way to attract voters who are not leftist—enough or should the party develop a more openly leftist agenda? Should social movements have a more structured relationship to it?

Movements and Questions

Beyond No and Beyond Exit

The entirely open questions facing Podemos are not unique to Spain's context. Of course, unlike in neighboring Portugal, or say, the United States, the energy of the streets found an institutional outlet in Podemos, and the party was quickly thrust into the limelight. But everywhere horizontalist movements have questioned traditional representative democracy and a similar set of questions has appeared.

Probably the most salient and divisive question has been about political parties. Should movements engage with them, and if so, on what basis? What can new political parties or new relationships to them look like? Some of the discussion is strategic. In the case of Spain, 15M's insistence on deliberation, civility, and internal democracy and its rejection of partisanship encouraged "non-activists" to join and play an important role. This gave it power and life at a time when leftist political parties could not attract participants even when social democratic parties were crumbling under their own bureaucratic structures. But it is hard to desire or even imagine complete disengagement from institutional politics, especially as institutions have tangible impact on so many pressing social justice issues for which there is no "exit strategy."

To the question of political parties we could add the related question of existing state institutions. As with the question of parties, there is often a tangible strategic knot. State institutions were not designed to enact "people power," but to protect powerful interests, to preserve the social order and its hierarchies, and to defend the sanctity of private property. But if the left does not engage institutional politics, our opponents will gladly do so, a task made especially easy in our absence. When we do engage, however, we often wind up legitimating and supporting a less-bad option, which may only provide (in the long run anyway) a slower path to the same bad destiny. These arguments play out today to infinite regress in many contexts. When we think about Occupy and the issues it faced and criticisms sometimes directed at it, we see the same concerns: the movement needed more concrete proposals, more institutional allies, and more tangible targets.

Behind the strategic question of political parties there is an even more difficult normative question, which has to do with how to think about representation in the first place. Many movements are leaderless, with a careful attention to the importance of spokespeople as opposed to leaders. The act of "speaking for" is treated carefully as the political act it is, or in some cases avoided entirely. Methods of direct democracy are preferred to representative ones. Direct participation is valued over indirect methods of delegating authority. Political parties are institutions of representation within a formal political arena.

But the language of group identity—race, gender, ethnicity, and class, for example, which has been so central to social justice struggles—implies an act of representation. The very act of claiming an identity, of a group demanding that it be *seen* and *recognized,* however, is often a powerful corrective. Social justice movements recognize this. The march toward a more egalitarian future is not derailed by these interruptions as much as recalibrated, the destination changed, made more precise. But, some argue, these acts of speaking for, of representation, are always imperfect, always partial, always vulnerable to capture and instrumental use. The question of representation mirrors the knot about institutional engagement and political parties: must we live in a world of necessary evils, of least-bad options, of flawed solutions, of slippery slopes toward mediocrity?

One answer—more popular and certainly more eloquent, developed by other authors—is to abandon the whole business altogether. This world is not made for us. So no representation, no identities, no parties, no institutions: Exit.

A different tack altogether is to think more deeply about what it means to radicalize our conception of democracy: to think about "Our Democracy" as opposed to "theirs," to think about the way that outside strategies can provide a counterweight to inside routes, for example. As I explore this alternative in the following pages, the lesson is not so much whether unions or organized indigenous federations should play explicit roles in broad formations, or if there should be gender set-asides in radical parties. The lesson is that we need to take up the challenge of "upgrading democracy" (as one of the 15M slogans went) and think about what that might mean in different contexts, as an ever-broadening swath of people become empowered protagonists over greater and greater domains of the world around them: the exact opposite of Exit.

2

We, the Sovereign

Popular sovereignty, in broad terms, refers to the people's rule, this only a more pointed version of the idea of democracy itself. Democracy is, as political theorists have long argued, fundamentally ambiguous on at least two principal questions: Who is entitled to govern? Who are the people on behalf of whom governing decisions should be made? Liberal approaches do not help us very much. Democracy, as usually discussed in liberal terms, is hard to define, and is usually defined against what it is *not*. Democracy is the rule of the *demos*, is usually the first answer one might arrive at. If pushed, the answer will continue: the *demos* is the political community; democracy is opposed to *theo*cracy, the rule of religious leaders, or *techno*cracy, the rule of experts, and so on.

No one quite knows where the demos should

end, and what rule by the demos should actually and specifically entail. To define these terms more specifically would get us into precisely the kind of terrain that liberal theory tries to avoid. To answer them in satisfactory ways invariably gets you into questions of inequality, egalitarianism, distribution, and power, which seem political, and it is important that liberal democracy maintain its pretense that it is neutral towards politics.

Popular sovereignty in a radically democratic vein, on the other hand, is more specific. This political theory means radicalizing answers to two questions: Who makes up the We? And how do We rule? The most radical answer to these questions implies a demos that is open, inclusive, egalitarian, and self-referential, while exerting sovereignty that is absolute over all relevant decisions that affect the conditions of life of the demos itself. And these two must always work together: the We placing a check on Sovereignty, while Sovereignty gives the We more meaning.

In other words, an emphasis on either the side of the We or of the Sovereign is incomplete. A project for popular sovereignty must always incorporate both concerns and place them in productive tension. As attractive as turning our back on existing institutions can seem at times (to focus on the We), this can be both dangerous and irresponsible, as it implies abandoning crucial issues on one hand but also leaving the most vulnerable among us behind, those who cannot be fugitives, who are trapped by institutions. The theory also implies, though, that an exclusive focus on rule (on being Sovereign) can turn movements into enforcers of bureaucratic agendas and amplifiers of oppressive common sense, or worse, justifiers of unjustifiable actions in the name of the left.

It is against this vanishing point where the two vectors meet that we assess our political projects, our movements, and our institutions. It is, more than anything, a set of coordinates that has helped activists navigate complicated terrains that accompany engaging with formal institutions, with political parties, and with coalitions. It is not meant to be a substitute for hard-nosed political economic analysis, nor is it a ready-to-use set of strategies or blueprints. That is, it is *not* synonymous with assemblies, democratic federations, or participatory councils. Those are among the many institutional forms it can take. And most important, popular sovereignty is also inherently tension-filled and contradictory. It needs to be thought of as a process more than an end state. Not only can sovereignty and democracy come into conflict, the whole project of popular sovereignty implies transforming institutions designed for other purposes and deeply structured by existing inequalities.

Liberal democracy, the dominant political framework of democracy today, one promoted by international agencies and powerful countries alike, emerged with capitalism and is its political mirror. It is a political version of free market economic theories. Its central tenets are the political equality, rights, and freedom of individuals before a minimal state that serves those individuals. It is a theory without concern for equality (beyond formal, individual political equalities) because to talk of egalitarianism imperils individual rights to property; it is a theory without concern for collective identities and the way they might exert power on the state (again, as this threatens individual property rights); and it is a theory that pretends it is politically neutral, even though it is only compatible with a free market. Liberal democracy is a theory that, in fact, is compatible with a vast range of inequalities and relies on the sanctity of individual rights to justify vast injustices in the name of free institutions and individuals. And it has precious little to say about the power of the people to rule over the conditions of their own lives.

Popular sovereignty pushes the other way. It radicalizes the meaning of democracy, insisting on the idea of the people as an egalitarian collective and the people's rule as a broad mandate to bring about social transformation. It politicizes the very issues that liberal democracy wishes to ignore.

The We

The first element to be addressed is about the makeup of the "We." In general terms, the makeup of "the people" is a political project. Politicians, nationalist leaders, social movements, constitutions, religious leaders all speak of "the people" and propose different projects for who properly belongs to "the people," who is at the center, and what the qualities and attributes of "the people" are. Right-wing populist leaders speak of "the people" in racist and xenophobic ways, drawing sharp boundaries on who properly belongs in the nation and declaring war on outsiders within.

But "the people" can be invoked in expansive ways as well: the anti-imperialist slogan "¡El pueblo unido jamás será vencido!" ("The people united shall never be defeated!"—originally a campaign slogan for Salvador Allende's 1970 campaign) has travelled the world from protest to protest because it invites us to think of a people that is expansive, that is egalitarian, that grows as it unites, and that is able to defeat powerful elites.

In the context of Latin America, the "We" of radically democratic projects was understood as a "historical bloc of the oppressed," made up of workers, the urban poor, peasant farmers, the landless, indigenous people, Afro-descendants; it is a people that comes into being through historical struggle for their lives, livelihood, rights, and recognition. Because Latin America did not fit European patterns of development, the thinking went, revolutionary movements might have more eclectic combinations than that of only an organized, industrial proletariat at its center, as more traditional Marxist theory would have had it. So different categories of actors, in the context of specific struggles, joined this bloc, as might allies, like intellectuals, university students, and urban professionals.

But the thinking went beyond that, as more struggles became visible: feminist movements, gay and lesbian movements, trans movements, movements of the differently abled. Each kind of movement or claim that makes itself visible has the possibility of interrupting the common sense about exactly who "the people" are, and this is an important source of renewal. In contrast to the endless debates about "identity politics vs. socialism" that preoccupied North American and European thinkers in the 1990s and 2000s, this tended to be much less fraught in Latin America (though, of course not without friction or resistance on the part of leadership as particular claims were made). Even if the leadership of the left on the continent did not manage, as a whole, to shed a white, male, and university-educated bias, it can be safely said that it is almost impossible to find, among leftist Latin American intellectuals of the era, screeds against black liberation or indigenous liberation, or feminism. And the sneer with which "identity politics" is sometimes said on the left in the United States, for example, would have been impossible to find.

The radical democratic position is nonetheless clear: the "We" that lines up to represent the people as a bloc against oppression and for emancipation is always somewhat partial; it has the oppressed at its center, and new movements and claims rooted in concrete struggles are an important part of its constant renewal. In Latin America, this bloc was broadly oriented by class, even if not strictly rooted in the industrial proletariat. The poor, the dispossessed, the marginalized, and the excluded move from the edges of society to its center to be the agents of its transformation. Popular capacity and agency are absolutely central to this account.

A second important element is that it is among social movements and in struggles for social justice that new imaginations about the world we want can and do appear. Not only might groups prefigure new social relationships, they might glimpse, in their cooperation and in their struggle, alternative futures. Various groups' capacity to imagine new worlds can transcend existing patterns of thought and behavior in any one group, even if in the social world we otherwise live in, we are severely limited in our ability to think beyond it. Everything, from the language we use to unspoken norms, is deeply conditioned by the inequalities of our social world; so is our imagination. Bringing very different people together as co-equals in struggle shakes up those possibilities.

We live in capitalist societies deeply structured by racial and gender inequalities. Much of Latin America is best described as an apartheid society, extremely violent and sexist, dependent on the subjugation of indigenous and Afro-descendant peoples alongside primitive forms of accumulation and resource extraction. Social movements do not so much provide an "outside" to that world as spaces to struggle against it, and there, in practice, to act "as if" it were egalitarian. Political projects involve both imagining new worlds and bringing them to life. Again, the radical democratic position is that autonomous social movements—or spaces free from the fetters of bureaucratic mandates that work to actively name and bracket the hierarchies we inherit—provide ideas, imagination, and creativity necessary for emancipatory political projects.

A third element of this position is that the "We" is both egalitarian *and* subject to a democratic referent: an imaginary and counterfactual standard of what a "true" democracy is, against which we can check ourselves. In Latin America, participants in these movements were always asking themselves if participation within this bloc was truly egalitarian: that is, whether people were equally valued and whether different voices and kinds of knowledge were valued. Remember that this was a bloc of the oppressed intent on social transformation, and inspired by popular education and liberation theology. The democratic referent was not some liberal notion of political equality of individuals, but rather closer to something that today we might call intersectional. Elite knowledge and voices did not have to be valued. The concern was rather with issues such as whether women spoke or had leadership positions; if indigenous knowledge was valued; if discussions were framed in popular language instead of elite, academic framings; or why the leadership of leftist movements or parties so often wound up being white men.

Even if movements start as leaderless, many times leaders emerged anyway, which is why procedures were put in place to hold them in check. Egalitarian *does not mean structureless*, and many realized in practice what movements around the world often come to: that structurelessness in fact tends to reproduce the privilege of some, but in insidious and unspoken ways. This was especially true as movements and coalitions scaled up and became more complex. So with them grew committees, representatives, delegates, these and other structures, with often very complex procedures for accountability and rotation. For some political formations within the left in Latin America in the 1990s, this democraticness was in fact what ultimately made them different from the region's populist movements of old.

So, what does it mean for the people to operate democratically? Some theorists have—mostly not successfully, in my view—attempted to then define what counts as democratic procedure by limiting it to a set of universal procedures, such as deliberation, a set of institutions like assemblies, or listing qualities (arguments based on reason, representation of particular groups). But just thinking of Latin America alone, what might be a democratic procedure for a union hall in the south of Brazil would be very different than for a village council in Zapatista territory. The self-questioning democratic referent simply varies from place to place and from time to time and evolves with the political project of emancipation. There are, of course, several questions that can be asked about the structure of the movement and its decision-making. Who actually participates? Are there features of these participatory spaces that prevent them from being open to all? Are there systematic biases about who speaks, and who decides? Is the technical language made accessible to all? But the bigger question is *whether power rests with some or with all in the historic bloc.* Movements that speak in the name of the people but that have entrenched leadership, hierarchical structures that prevent innovation or rotation, or that operate in a top-down manner do not meet the radical democratic standard of a "We."

We, the Sovereign

The Importance of Sovereignty

So far the account of a radically democratic "We" does not sound very different than what many contemporary social movements already do. Thinking of a historic bloc of the oppressed that resists closure, that prefigures the world we want in its creativity, and that is egalitarian and democratic could be a description of the "99 percent" that Occupy sought to construct, for example. But popular sovereignty does not rest only in the making of a radically democratic people. It is also constituted by the political construction of self-rule by those people. This leads us to the second component of the theory, which refers to the coupling of that "We" with empowered decision-making. Or, as I am calling it here, sovereignty.

Sovereignty is a central component of democracy. Without sovereignty, without the people's rule, democracy is an empty exercise. Dominant views of democracy try to avoid discussions of sovereignty most of the time. A radical view of democracy, popular sovereignty, insists on it, and insists on more demanding standards. It means insisting that the people *really* rule, and that they rule *over all decisions that affect their lives*. This, no less than an egalitarian and radically democratic "We," is a utopian vanishing point. It also means asking if the rule is exposed to the democratic referent. Is it the radically democratic "We" that exerts the rule, and is the act of ruling further democratizing society? But what was the attraction of sovereignty, of ruling, for movements that were born outside the state?

First was that many of the urgent demands of social movements required decisive state action. To indigenous nations in the region, sovereignty meant both the right to self-determination and freedom from colonialism. Indigenous conceptions of sovereignty, which were not always coterminous with nation-states, evolved over the years in a tense dynamic with the colonial and neocolonial states. Indigenous communities re-appropriated and re-deployed the state's organizational and legal forms, in ways that ultimately strengthened the indigenous movement's ability to contest state policies.

In addition, Latin America and its social fabric were thought to be so shaped by colonialism and inequality that simply winning the palace and opening up its doors to societal influence was thought not to be enough, as, for example, the civil society theorists might imagine would be the case in a democratized Eastern Europe. In Latin America, in contrast, the analysis was that the state needed to be enlisted both to democratize society and to set up institutionalized links for popular influence in absence of those pre-existing networks. Analysts of the time recognized that the state and its structures were shaped by the ruling class, and that it would be important to transform state institutions while mobilizing sources of popular counter-power in order to face inevitable ruling-class resistance.

The first concern is to ask, pointedly and specifically, if the people *actually* rule, and if they rule over *the issues that matter to them*. Many of these countries were transitioning to democracy, and some had been formal democracies for some time. In principle, people "ruled," albeit indirectly. Citizens went to the ballot box to select politicians from a group of political parties no doubt made up of elites. No matter who won, those winners would install political appointees who would work with career bureaucrats to enact policies that were not in the interests of the majority, and whose parameters of discussion were infinitely narrower than the ideas that were emerging, for example, among movements. Specifically, then, popular sovereignty insists that we ask: are there institutionalized, direct, and transparent links between the "We" and government action? Do the parameters of questions match the imagination that emerges among movements? What discretion do elected officials, technical staff, and bureaucrats have over popular decisions once they are made?

A second concern for a radical view of sovereignty is if people actually rule over *all decisions* that matter to them and impact their life. One of the problems that plagued Latin American democracies—and plague democracies in the Global North today—is that what is subject to decision-making power via formal democratic mechanisms is infinitely smaller than the set of decisions that impact people's lives. In fact, given the market fundamentalism we live under today, it might be argued that the more irrelevant a decision is, the more scope for action there is over it. And many issues of extreme importance have layers of authority that escape national jurisdictions; to renationalize water, as happened in Bolivia in 2003, was an act carried out in national territory but it impinged on property rights in other countries and had repercussions in international courts. Increasingly, popular sovereignty needs to reach in the direction of international domains for issues that might seem local.

Finally, the radical view of sovereignty asks if the act of ruling is carried out under the orientation of the people, and is it done in a democratizing way? A radical view of sovereignty demands that there be a system of constant checks to provide democratic and popular oversight over the policies and over those carrying them out. Magnanimous acts on behalf of the poor are not democratic, and even seemingly egalitarian impulses need to be checked when they come from central institutions, as they create a passive version of equality. National literacy campaigns may look like harmless measures, but not if they devalue native languages or popular ways of speaking, and not if they are done without grassroots leadership. This implies asking not only if the act of ruling is being carried out under democratic will, but also if every act of rule further democratizes society. Just as the democratic referent of the "We" would be open to constant reinvention, what sovereignty implies would also change over time.

Popular sovereignty needs to be conceived as an ongoing process, a project that is always going to be incomplete and open to constant renewal. For this reason it is important to tell its story not as an abstract set of principles, but as instantiated in specific movements and concrete struggles, where the balancing act it requires can be seen in action. In the next chapters I discuss how this has taken place in Latin America in the last two decades.

3

Social Movement Parties

If "they" do not represent us, who can? Conventional wisdom dictates that political parties on the left are bound to disappoint at some stage. Leftist thinking on the party question is haunted by a long history of hope and disappointment for much of the twentieth century. Whether we are speaking of Eastern European Communist parties or more recent examples such as South Africa's ANC, among others, the fears that bureaucratization, hierarchy, corruption, and censorship are inherent features of political parties seem well founded.

For movements premised on the idea that "they do not represent us," and oriented around the ideals of direct democracy, the very idea of a formalized structure of political representation seems paradoxical but unavoidable. The challenge, of course, has not deterred activists in recent years from wanting to reinvent or at least reinvigorate the very idea of political parties, be it through Spain's Podemos, Germany's Die Linke, Greece's Syriza, or Turkey's HDP. There is no doubt that today's movements need new structures of political representation beyond the existing political party landscape in most countries. The question before us today is what political parties might look like under radically democratic coordinates.

It is worth revisiting the Latin American experience with leftist parties in the 1980s and 1990s, when the idea of a *social movement party* emerged, one that was both novel and for a time quite successful. Instead of a party of cadres in which social movements provide the shock troops (and votes) for a party led by an enlightened leadership, the traditional vanguardism of the Cuban CP of the time, the direction was supposed to flow the other way —"leading by following," as the Zapatista slogan said.

In all, it was a vision of representation anchored in popular sovereignty, one in which the transformation of institutions and the people took place at the same time. Social movement parties were understood as vehicles to translate social movement energies and ideas into platforms and policies that would further democratize society. The plurality, energy, and creativity from movements was supposed to keep political parties from becoming the empty and self-serving bureaucratic shells activists saw when they gazed at Eastern Europe.

In this section I turn to this generation of experimentation in Latin America for what it might say to today's activists, briefly touching on the early days of Brazil's Workers' Party (PT) and of the Bolivian Movement for Socialism (MAS), discussing these parties: political formations both rooted in, and in principle driven by, social movements. Of course, I write these words with the benefit of hindsight, and the stories also give rise to significant caution. Many of these political parties successfully entered national political arenas, tilting the whole regional political balance to the left in the 2000s. The overall balance of the so-called Pink Tide is decidedly a mixed one, one of material gains for the poor but also the transformation of these parties away from the guidance of social movements as they entered national arenas. I will draw principally on the move of Brazil's Workers' Party away from its radical roots toward a more hierarchical and traditional model as a cautionary tale that reflects broader tendencies.

We, the Sovereign

Lessons from Another Moment

In the 1980s, just when Margaret Thatcher was famously repeating that "there is no alternative to free markets," activists in Latin America were beginning to experiment with exactly such alternatives. New forms of left politics arose, such as that in Villa El Salvador, Peru, an early and ambitious experiment in collective self-governance rooted in liberation theology, indigenous principles, and flexible Marxism. In the 1990s, when the UK's Labour Party and the US Democratic Party were taking major ideological turns to the right, Latin America's new left was making important electoral and social gains, forging coalitions around plural political subjects. By the 2000s (when Thatcher's argument seemingly no longer even needed to be made in the Global North) the Latin American continent as a whole was electing left-of-center governments that emerged from those new political parties. The Pink Tide brought to presidential power a remarkable cohort of activists throughout the region—including former union leaders, radical indigenous activists, former guerrilla fighters, and liberation theologians.

But in retrospect, Latin America in the 1980s and 1990s would not seem fertile ground for such new politics. Just as military dictatorships were giving way to formal democracies, Structural Adjustment Programs and other forms of fiscal austerity were being introduced. Hyperinflation, unsustainable debt payments, and the loss of purchasing power for working and middle classes were central to the day-to-day realities of Latin Americans of the 1980s. Urban areas *nearly doubled* in population as peasants were forced off the land due to World Bank / IMF–mandated major infrastructural projects and the legacy of authoritarian developmentalism.

The 1990s brought stability, but economic liberalization continued. This resulted in greater social inequality as well as more intensive environmental exploitation, as states and regions competed to attract foreign investment. The decline in public-sector spending and the restructuring of industrial manufacturing further exacerbated the gap between the haves and have-nots. By the end of the 1990s the wealthy could create some of the trappings of world-level consumption in cities such as Caracas and São Paulo, but did so from behind the confines of secluded buildings and gated enclaves. At the same time, neoliberal reforms coupled with the drive to export primary commodities meant the aggressive opening up of agricultural frontiers and exploitation of natural resources, including the privatizing of natural resources like water and natural gas.

The result of all of these changes—ever-sharper social cleavages and the impoverishment of the majority, environmental degradation, expropriation of indigenous and peasant lands, straining urban infrastructure and social apartheid in elite cities—only fueled the mobilization of social movements. Social movements appeared throughout the region to contest some of these conditions and the policies behind them. These ranged from unions struggling against poor working conditions, to urban movements fighting for access to housing and urban services, to indigenous movements demanding autonomy and peasant movements demanding access to land, among others.

Because this took place in the context of the emergence of basic democratic guarantees and the increasing salience of local arenas as sites of political contestation, movement activists had the opportunity to engage institutions and form new alliances, often at the local level. After the dictatorships, new civilian governments strengthened formal democratic institutions and in principle guaranteed some elementary protections of freedom of speech and political opposition. Many countries also engaged in processes of administrative devolution and decentralization, as this was part of a new emerging international development consensus, to bring local governments "closer to the population." This converged with many movements' increasingly local focus.

Traditional leftist parties (such as the older Communist parties or their factional offspring) of the region were unable to represent these new emergent demands, unwilling to engage in electoral contests, and too organizationally weak given the previous decades of repression under military regimes. Certainly not all social movements engaged with political parties, but the ones that did had to reinvent the very idea of a party, sometimes rejecting the term entirely.

Some inspiration for the new parties came from European debates, such as the "march toward socialism in peace and freedom" line from Italian and Spanish Communist Parties, or the German Green Party's "one foot in and one foot out" of institutions position. If in Europe the so-called Eurocommunist debates were (for some) the death-knell of a vision of radical transformation of society, in contexts such as Latin America they opened vast new vistas for Marxist-inspired thought and practice. And these new parties were also clearly Latin American. Liberation theology, the re-interpretation of Catholic doctrine to emphasize the liberation of the oppressed, was extremely influential. And so was popular education, the pedagogical movement associated with Paulo Freire. A combination of anti-colonial and Marxist thought, this was an approach to education that simultaneously valorized the voices and agency of the oppressed while proposing that liberation was the goal of educational praxis. Also important were generations of radical Latin American thinkers who had argued for the value of Latin American ideas. The memory of indigenous struggles such as the Katari uprising in Bolívia in the eighteenth century were extremely important, as were indigenous concepts such as the Inca idea of *ayni*, meaning cooperation, or *tekojoja*, the Guaraní concept of justice, or *sumak kawsay*, the Quechua conception of living in harmony (sometimes translated as *buen vivir*, living well). Two of the paradigmatic cases in Latin America are Brazil's Workers' Party and Bolivia's Movement toward Socialism, or the PT and MAS, as they usually known.

Where Movements Could Speak: Brazil's PT

Brazil's Workers' Party, or PT (Partido dos Trabalhadores) was formally founded in 1980 by a group of union and social movement leaders,

Catholic activists, members of revolutionary left-ist organizations, and intellectuals in an effort to seize on the new social movement energies on the eve of the country's transition to democracy. The discussion about what sort of left political formation should emerge had been going on for some time. The increasingly militant labor move-ment (the "new unionism" of the time) was, more and more, emphasizing autonomy from the official union structures, often infiltrated by and subject to manipulation by corporatist arrangements. This union movement was meanwhile showing off its new might at a series of spectacular strikes in the country's main industrial areas. At the same time, unionists were increasingly working in concert with community-based movements, themselves often under the influence of liberation theology. The stu-dent movement and urban rights movements were also stepping up their activities at the time.

If there was agreement that the older models were not adequate, there were disagreements as to whether the new party should be narrowly class-oriented or have a broader social base; whether it should privilege electoral victories or social trans-formation; whether it should formally represent unions; whether it should focus on shop-floor victories or on building political power; whether it should treat democratic institutions instrumentally or as ends unto themselves; whether it should be internally plural, and if so, how it should treat internal divergences, and so on. And much of the debate took place between these extremes.

In the end, the pervasive ethos of popular education and liberation theology won the day. The new political party was not only a new kind of party but a new structure of political representation, premised on respect for popular knowledge and voices. From its inception it privileged radical democracy over staid slogans, and sought to incorporate social movements without co-opting them. This was a socialist party with a plural system of internal tendencies that defended democratic institutions and the rule of law, and brought together a rainbow of social movements and identities under its banner. Rejecting much of what came before it, the new party was united under the principles of movement autonomy, a commitment to democratic institutions and internal democracy, a mass base, and socialism.

One of the central ideas of the PT was that the party would provide a common political space to articulate various popular struggles while respecting the autonomy of all movements. This was to be a broad-based coalition under a socialist program, combining the interests of labor with those of wider social bases. A party where "social movements could speak," as the phrase went, was envisioned as a plural party that gave political and institutional expression to civil society. The idea of a social movement party meant that from the start it maintained close relationships with a spate of popular movements that ranged from more urban and middle-class groups, such as human rights and environmental groups, to rural and peasant groups, such as the landless movement. And in spite of its roots in labor, the PT did not establish a formal institutional relationship with unions, nor was it controlled or funded by unions. In fact, the party's funding originally came from membership dues (set at a minimum cost of a *cafezinho*, a cup of coffee, per month). It was common for party members to maintain multiple affiliations at one time, often belonging to a movement as well as to the party. Particularly in those early days, party ideology was often a heady mix of anti-capitalism, workerism, radical democracy, class-coalition consciousness, and liberation theology.

Another of the distinctive features of PT practice and ideology was its "vocation to govern." This did not necessarily mean that it would privilege electoral contests but that it saw transformation of institutions as both a goal and a strategy. This is no doubt related to the fact that it emerged in large urban centers and that social movement activists who had been mobilizing around urban rights, such as transportation, had ideas about how to improve the running of those services through user councils. Some of the first ideas emerged from activists who had been involved in user councils for public health clinics in São Paulo. Health activists demanded that users have a say in how public clinics were run through these councils, which became, in turn, powerful spaces for organizing and for consciousness-raising activities. Popular education conversations on the problems of a particular clinic could lead to discussions on patriarchy, capitalism, and the role of the state. In other words, this was not narrowly about service delivery but about bettering people's material conditions as one triumph in the development of a broader class coalition for socialism.

A model of internal democracy arose. In addition to the principle of listening to movements without co-opting them, the party had two additional, important elements that were supposed to function as a check against bureaucratization. First was a complex system of party branches and direct elections. Party branches were given broad autonomy to set directives, and particularly in the early days were often more involved with extra-institutional struggles. The distinction between party and constituent social organizations was blurred and the party, through its local branches, appeared more as a movement, or an umbrella of movements, engaged on a variety of fronts. Local branches were deeply shaped by local struggles, so in some places industrial workers might be more prominent, but in another environmentalists and peasant farmers would dominate. And the party provided campaign support to local elections, emphasizing always the development of new leadership. Second, there was a system of internal "tendencies," or internal factions that would compete ideologically within the party, while working together externally. A system of "proportional representation" within party directorates was meant to guarantee the voice of minority factions. The idea was to keep the party nimble, with competition between tendencies as a check on bureaucratic pressures.

Though born as a "party of social movements," in the 1990s the PT garnered successes in governing local administrations through participatory mechanisms. In the country's first free elections in 1988, Brazilians elected PT mayors in 36 cities, bringing an unprecedented *10 percent* of the population under PT administrations. In what was later described as the party's first "shock of reality," several of these ended disastrously, as newly elected mayors faced difficult choices as they tried to negotiate competing political pressures from local elites, higher levels of government, and challenges from the party's own base.

The questions that had dogged the party's formation now seemed to come back: should the party run administrations for workers, or for whole cities? Should the party occupy local administrations in order to win national office, or should it administer for its own sake? In some cases elected mayors from the PT came into open conflict with municipal workers' unions that had propelled them into office. In other cases, there were sharp conflicts between municipal party directorates and administrators from the party. In the city of São Paulo, which had once been imagined as a "flagship" PT administration, a *nine-day* strike by municipal bus drivers (one of the worst in the city's history) a few months before the election paralyzed the metropolis, polarized local party activists, and seemed to doom the party's electoral ambitions. Similarly poignant stories played out in other cities that had once been union and PT strongholds.

Fortunes turned around, though, by the late 1990s. The mayors from the PT who came into office in 1997 arrived with a new set of tools and ideas forged from experimentation over the previous years. The political goals of the party remained the same, but the strategy now was less reliant on organized sectors and more on unorganized popular voices who were to have a say in local government through mechanisms of participation. Apart from participation in budgets, PT administrations thus experimented with countless institutional forms of participation: through education, through health, and through councils focusing on women, the elderly, Afro-Brazilians, youth, human rights, and many other topics. A central component of this participation was its connection with *real decision-making*, always under a broad strategy of social transformation and redistribution. It prided itself on running clean and transparent local administrations.

The party continued to grow, and in city after city it was able to run effective administrations while attracting new members from outside of the social movement and union sectors that had been central to its founding. By the late 1990s it seemed to have done something unimaginable just two decades before: it maintained a socialist platform, it continued to support different social struggles, and it managed to grow in its appeal to unorganized sectors, both among the poor and increasingly to middle classes, owing in particular to its successes at administration. It had an organizational presence in most cities in the country by that time, and had hundreds of thousands of active members. The party's ascent to national prominence and its electoral victory in 2002 would pose another set of challenges altogether, however, which I discuss below.

Not a Party, a Political Instrument: Bolivia's MAS

The Assembly for the Sovereignty of the Peoples (ASP) was officially formed in 1995, fifteen years after Brazil's PT, and would assume its current name of MAS–IPSP (Movement toward Socialism—Political Instrument of Popular Sovereignty), or simply MAS, in 1999. This movement-party represents another solution to the problem of political representation of social movements. If the PT was imagined as a party where "movements could speak," it was still very much a political party, with strong institutional mechanisms to both allow movements to speak and to preserve internal party democracy. Part of this was to preserve the autonomy of movements. The MAS was always less institutionalized than the PT, and was founded with a greater emphasis on organic relationships to social movements rather than formal party structures; it was also less tied to the idea of the political party itself, defining itself as an "instrument" to be overcome; and it owed much less to European debates on socialism and democracy than to decolonial ideas and indigenous political philosophies in combination with Marxism.

The MAS was, very much like the PT, a party borne of radical social and labor movements, though in this case majority indigenous and rural ones. Bolivia is nearly two-thirds indigenous, with sharp racial boundaries defining much of social life. In the years since its founding, rural social movements and unions had been agitating against neoliberal policies of austerity whose brunt was being borne by the already impoverished indigenous majority. Sometimes the demands were articulated as class demands and sometimes in terms of indigenous rights and recognition.

In the mid-1980s, Bolivia closed down several of its state-owned mining enterprises, which had been a site of militant union activity for several decades. Thousands of displaced miners went into coca-farming regions, adding to the growing militancy there, bringing with them both organizational capacity and socialist ideology. The coca growers' union, despite repression, fought to keep coca production legal and developed a high level of political organization. Other displaced miners went to the city of El Alto, where they formed autonomous mutual assistance associations.

In 1994, the Popular Participation Law created over 300 new governments and indigenous and rural movements began to engage these, with varying degrees of success. But social movements did not want only local participation; bigger goals were sovereignty and the right to self-determination. In that same year, a federation of coca-farmer and peasant unions, the Assembly for the Sovereignty of the People (ASP), formed a "political instrument" that was essentially an arm of the federation, to run candidates and make demands. For procedural reasons, in 1999 it wound up officially adopting the name MAS–IPSP, MAS being an acronym for a political party that was no longer active at the time.

While the first elections in which it participated produced tangible results in rural areas of Cochabamba (the center of coca-farmer activism), by 1997 it had managed to elect Evo Morales, a union leader, to Parliament. At the time, these were all-volunteer electoral campaigns without outside sources of funding; candidates themselves had to contribute two months' salary. Local chapters self-produced campaign materials such as flags and T-shirts that were used to raise funds. The "political instrument" at its start was essentially an extension of the federation, and there was no party structure per se. Local union chapters decided on their candidates, and the central coordinating committee oversaw the whole process. General assemblies made party decisions, which were then passed down to local chapters for ratification.

Nonetheless the successes of those first elections occasioned a lot of re-thinking about what this new party should be: should it be a rural-only party or extend to urban sectors? An indigenous party or a pro-indigenous party? Should it formalize or remain an "instrument"? Should it have national ambitions or remain a regional party?

At the time of the name change, the MAS began to set its sights on becoming a radical opposition party inside the electoral system and to expand its base socially and geographically. Over the next few years, the MAS extended its operations to actively incorporate autonomous movements into the party, which then began its evolution into the multi-class rural and urban pro-indigenous national party that it would become. The so-called Water Wars of 2000 (when water in Cochabamba was privatized and handed to a multinational and then renationalized after protests), and the Gas War of 2003 (a plan to cheaply sell Bolivian gas to Chilean and American intermediaries) were real victories for increasingly emboldened social movements, with the MAS now playing a more visible role.

MAS leaders brokered important alliances, sometimes bringing movement leaders directly into its structures, and sometimes seeking to occupy leadership positions in movements. It also capitalized on opportunities, like the earlier collapse of a rival opposition party in El Alto, to position itself as the main voice of oppositional movements and sentiments in Bolivia. Much like the PT in Brazil, the MAS relied on successful local administrations—ones that were participatory, well-governed, with a reputation for governing well, and capable of developing a loyal base of voters as they managed re-election. In 1999 the MAS elected 10 mayors, mostly in Cochabamba, while by 2004, it elected 95 throughout the country.

It opened its doors to an extremely broad membership, including university students and urban professionals. Small leftist factions and urban environmentalist groups joined as well. But in doing so, the MAS underwent a profound transformation: it opened up membership and candidate lists to individuals, and not just members of unions. This meant that the MAS developed a party structure, even if it still understood itself as an "instrument" (and operated as such in its home region of rural Cochabamba). Party officials now, for example, directly mobilized masses and ran meetings to decide on candidates, particularly in urban areas, functions that might have been previously carried out by movements. In other words, if the MAS continued to operate in its original, bottom-up, movement-driven way in rural areas, its mobilization elsewhere was party-driven. Activists worried at the time about opportunistic infiltration by middle-class segments; they were also concerned that the development of a party structure that directly mobilized members might now be used to outweigh movements within the MAS. Some radical movements felt they were instrumentally used for legitimacy in electoral contests.

Even if it was a fraught structure, it was an electorally successful one. In 2005, with this plural coalition, hybrid structure, and a broad socialist and pro-indigenous platform, the MAS won national elections, making Morales the country's first indigenous president. At his inauguration in 2006, Morales famously invoked the Katari uprising, Simon Bolívar, Che Guevara, and Subcomandante Marcos of the Zapatistas, while promising to re-found the nation along indigenous socialist lines. It was a platform of national socialist transition, collective ownership of natural resources, anti-imperialism, popular democracy, and the indigenous rights to self-determination that remained at its core.

It is hard to overstate the significance of the electoral victory. Evo Morales became the country's first indigenous president in this apartheid society, and the winner of the country's first outright electoral majority since 1952. From its founding to its entrance into the presidential palace, the MAS achieved in ten years what had eluded socialist parties elsewhere for many generations, while drawing on a lineage of 500 years of indigenous struggles on the continent. It used the ballot box and the institutions of formal democracy to advance a movement goal of indigenous self-assertion. Shortly after its victory, the MAS initiated a series of popular democratic assemblies to re-write the country's constitution.

What has been more difficult for the MAS has been to navigate being an "instrument"—something that is both a social movement and a political party, particularly while in power. The outsized persona of Morales and the faithful allegiance to him is at odds with the party's horizontalist and democratic commitments. The MAS in power has had an

increasingly difficult time accepting social movement input and opposition when it conflicts with
the national government's priorities. This has been
particularly poignant going into Morales's second
and third terms, as I briefly detail below.

The Tension between Collectives and Individuals

One of the tensions throughout the history of
both parties involves the recognition of individuals
and collectives. Should a leftist structure of representation be based on a rainbow of groups and
identities, or should it be based on an egalitarian
and horizontal formation? There are profoundly
different principles in play, both of which have
a legacy on the left: one placing special value in
autonomous spaces and their capacity to generate demands and identities and the other placing
special value in spaces where all can participate
on an equal footing. If you recall, with Spain's
Indignados individuals spoke for themselves and
not in the name of political groups, movements,
or collective identities. MAS, in its early days, was
at the other extreme: the party was a federation of
movements that were represented within the party.
And the PT from its founding was somewhere

in the middle—it was a party where movements could speak, but it was from the start a party of individual members. Looking at Latin American left political parties of the 1980s and 1990s shows there is a constantly swinging pendulum between these two emphases.

Early on there was a lot of attention to ideas of "council democracy," the idea of special representation from existing organizations. But later, with electoral ambitions or successes, parties like the MAS or the PT sought the attention of the unorganized sectors of society. But this meant that political collectives such as unions, which were previously understood as privileged interlocutors, became symbolically reduced to a segment now much smaller than the whole. To accept individuals or to privilege direct forms of participation does not work *against* political collectives per se, but it does challenge their monopoly over representing the people, or the idea that they represent all.

From the point of view of popular sovereignty, there is no correct answer to this tension, only a recognition that the two principles represent different and necessary democratizing impulses that need to be activated at different times. An exclusive focus on collectives can harden those differences and entrench their leaderships; a focus on individuals might both weaken movements' abilities to challenge the party and not allow certain patterns of inequalities to be addressed within the party.

Keeping the Party in Check

Founding documents and debates of both the MAS and the PT have the implicit understanding that political parties are to some extent a necessary evil. A party as a structure of representation implies a certain amount of closure, while the radically democratic logic of movements tends to undermine it. How can a party operate in an existing democracy and remain accountable to its radical principles? If this is easier to imagine in a local social movement setting, it becomes much more complex in broader political arenas. Political parties accumulate knowledge, centralize information, and engage in activities that are impossible to constantly monitor, as well as having delegated structures.

The PT and the MAS sought slightly different solutions aimed at trying to prevent the party from "running away from its roots." Founders were also extremely concerned with preventing these parties from reverting to the default populist politics of the region. The history of Latin America is full of examples of mass mobilization, right *and* left, of movements and unions behind charismatic politicians who used them for legitimacy.

The architects of the PT sought to build a set of overt institutional checks to prevent these outcomes. These were principled commitments to social movement autonomy, the mechanisms of internal democracy, and competition between internal factions. The MAS, on the other hand, sought to be a more nimble structure—an "instrument"—that mirrored its founding movements. Organizationally, the party developed few rigid structures or positions, and leaders were supposed to be spokespeople. In contrast to the PT's complex system of locals and party congresses, there were only two top committees of the MAS where issues could be worked out, and both had rotating representatives from the base. If, in the case of the PT version, the downside of that model was a structural rigidity that could be captured by professionalized party elites, in the case of the MAS the problem was that movements could lose their autonomy and identity within the party.

Social Movement Parties

How Parties in Power Change

Neither the PT nor the MAS remained immune to pressures to change once in or near national power, and the lessons hold for many of the other Pink Tide parties that achieved national power. What may have seemed relatively straightforward at a local or regional level—to articulate a coalition behind a redistributive political project while retaining accountability to autonomous social movements—became unimaginably more complex nationally. Powerful moneyed interests line up in a much more disciplined way once issues such as nationalizing natural resources or imposing capital controls become real possibilities. The threat of capital flight or elite revolt limits the scope of government action. The very structure of the national state is more impermeable to change. And at the same time, the danger of a right-wing backlash seems to call for more caution and moderation on the government's part, and increasing calls from the government for allied movements to be cooperative. Coordinated international interference from business groups or the US is a possibility never far off.

And to complicate matters, movement activists come to occupy important positions in government, perhaps hollowing out social movements or threatening their autonomy. And with paid positions, and perhaps even direct government funding, movements can become dependent on the government's electoral fortunes in ways that impinge directly on livelihoods. Elected officials become less accountable in the name of expediency. The need to stay in power and pass legislation can lead elected officials to get involved in status-quo corrupt politics, which renders them even less accountable. And movements that were supposed to be a radicalizing counterweight to the party find themselves in the confusing position of having to *defend* ever more moderate policies against even worse conservative forces.

The specific story of the PT's drift away from its historic commitments to popular democracy over its first ten years in national government is one version of that account. The PT arrived in Brasilia in 2003 carrying with it not only the hopes and expectations of the country's poor majority, but also with two decades of experience with local administrations and Parliament. The expectation was that the administration would put people first, break with Brazilian corrupt ways of doing politics, and carry through a process of transforming Brazilian society and institutions. This democratic and socialist transition would give expression to the rainbow of movements that produced the historic victory that put a union activist in the presidency for the first time.

The very significant and real improvements in people's lives that came about from a dozen years of the PT in national power are undeniable. This includes a stark reduction in poverty owing to its cash transfer programs, a radical increase in access to all levels of education, especially higher education; the introduction, for the first time, of affirmative action policies in universities; and the construction of high numbers of permanent, affordable housing units for the poor, among other gains. But it is surprising how a party in national power became so vulnerable, so quickly, to deviations from its founding radically democratic principles. Not only did it capitulate to capitalist interests, it became much less accountable to social movements and organized sectors that came to be seen as subordinate to the party's leadership. In its first year, the PT backed a controversial set of pension reforms, which led to the departure of some historic founders of the party and the expulsion of PT parliamentarians who refused to fall in line. By 2005 the PT was involved in a major corruption scandal in Parliament—something unthinkable just a few years back when it was widely known as the party of ethical governance, and a symptom of how much the party had acquiesced to the status quo modes of politics.

Movements, which at first sought to pressure the administration from the left to provide legitimacy for a redistributive administration, became disillusioned about their ability to have a voice. National unions were expected, more and more, to play a supporting role. Even though the administration innovated in the sheer number of social movement activists hired into government, many of whom created new ministries and departments with genuine resources and capacities, it never shared power. At the end of Lula's first term, an oft-repeated phrase from the leadership of the Landless Workers' Movement echoed a collective sentiment in much of the movement sector, of "being better off with him than without him."

The party's mode of organizing changed during the period: instead of developing *militants*, it worried now about recruiting sheer numbers of *voters* for the administration and individual members. The party nearly doubled in members at the same time as internal rules were changed so as to weaken local chapters. And even if the administration was successful in delivering results for the poor, these were divorced from political work. Political work at the base, such as that organized by liberation theologians in urban peripheries in the 1980s and 1990s, ceased. Other sectors had similar experiences. Even though the numbers of university students doubled over the period, the number of students in the national student union did not increase; hundreds of thousands of families moved into permanent homes, but numbers of neighborhood associations did not increase; tens of millions of people joined the formal labor force, but union membership did not appreciably increase.

But changes were most apparent in the rupture with the principle of direct, popular input into decision-making, its strategic gamble on activating popular pressure as a way to generate legitimacy for redistributive projects. This gave way to a model of governance based on congressional compromise and consultative practices of "listening" and "dialogue." So even though the administration sponsored well-attended participatory forums on dozens of issues from LGBT rights to the environment and the elderly, they were divorced from impactful decision-making.

Instead of relying on organized and unorganized sectors for legitimacy, the national administration found itself seeking support in broad congressional coalitions with parties from the center and from the right. In doing so, it doled out posts to political allies and compromised on policy and legislation, yielding a national administration that was not only difficult to comprehend as a PT administration but that also lacked coherence. PT politicians increasingly engaged in traditional political practices of favor-trading and fundraising, despite repeated pleas from some parts of the party to "clean house." The June 2013 protests that brought the country to a standstill—originally a protest around the right to mobility by an autonomous leftist organization—showed that the party was disconnected from energies from the streets. By the time the protests morphed into a wave of elite and middle-class discontent with redistribution and leftism, it was hard to contain. The country's elites and its monopolistic media were then able to channel that resentment into support for a right-wing parliamentary coup that has not only undone several of the gains of the PT era but actually gone much further in privatizing public assets and undoing labor, environmental, and social protections of the last decades.

The case of the MAS is another illustrative story of the political transformation of a party in national power. As with the PT, the gains for the impoverished majority of Bolivia since Evo's victory in 2004 are undeniable. And, more noticeably than probably anywhere else in Latin America, we are seeing the beginnings of a settling of accounts of the historic wrongs of colonization. If the PT became a hardened structure that was difficult to hold accountable in national power, with the MAS, the lack of boundaries between movement, party, and governmental project meant that the very idea of autonomous movements critical of the government as anything other than an "enemy" of the popular project was hard to accept.

During Evo's first term, the MAS government promoted a historic participatory process of the rewriting of the constitution that would go on to describe the country as plurinational, recognizing the right to self-determination of indigenous nations within Bolivia, while also introducing indigenous quotas in government. In those early years, the MAS government also began a process of land reform, while having to come to a compromise with a right-wing separatist uprising in the lowlands. And although the MAS won the national administration twice more, its relationships with movements became increasingly fraught as it has more and more sought legitimacy with the electorate and made increasing compromises with elite interests and conservative parties. Government policies have tilted to the right while the party has not been able to renew its leadership and develop other nationally prominent figures of the stature of Evo—a real departure from the radically democratic principles behind the party.

The case of the planned highway in the TIPNIS national park (Territorio Indígena y Parque Nacional Isiboro Sécure) is well-known and telling. The government proposed and justified the plan in terms of regional economic development. Local indigenous groups protested the plan as unconstitutional since they had not been consulted. Other indigenous groups and social movements (many within the MAS) joined in solidarity, since the plan clearly violated the principles of indigenous self-determination and "protection of mother Earth" that the MAS officially espoused. Two of the original groups behind the MAS, including the powerful Confederation of Indigenous People of Bolivia (CIDOB), split with it in 2011 over this. The government dismissed protestors as factionalists, foreign agents, or tools of oligarchs. In a worrying turn, the government has increasingly framed oppositional movements, or simply movements that did not march in lockstep with the MAS, as enemies, even if officially welcoming movement criticism.

Social Movement Parties Are Still Needed

Similar criticisms exist of nearly all Pink Tide political parties. The game of national rule clearly exposes leftist party structures to pressures: to be expedient, to remain in power, to pass legislation, to make alliances in Congress, to ward off the right, to instrumentalize movements for legitimacy. The strategic question facing the next generation of leftist parties clearly will be how to face these pressures and how to scale up from local arenas. The recurring questions moving forward continue to concern the consequences of formalizing a structure of political representation from the point of view of popular sovereignty.

Parties can create crucial coordinating structures across movements, as movements contest political arenas at various scales and locations. Parties can provide crucial expertise, support, and resources to various struggles and put them in relationship to one another in the context of a broader struggle. Parties can provide concrete fantasies stitched together from various elements. But if movements are to provide this kind of creativity and energy to political parties, the relationship between them cannot be one in which political parties co-opt movements or draw them into the role of legitimating political platforms. Social movement parties, at their best, encouraged spaces in which unorganized citizens became discussants, but the quality of these spaces depended, somewhat ironically, on their autonomy from party control. Sometimes observers from the Global North are surprised to find the fluid merging of class, ethnic, and popular identities in social justice struggles in Latin America, but they seldom look at the political parties that make this merging possible. The intersectionalism that observers sometimes find so admirable seldom happened by itself—it appeared in the context of a broad, transformative vision of social justice.

It is important that political parties be constantly exposed to the radical democratic referent: is it leading by following? Does it express the rule of the few or the many? Are there mechanisms and checks in place to protect this internal democracy? And given that parties have had so many difficulties once in national power, what checks are there to protect its internal democracy (and autonomy of constituent movements) in that case? How can party bases recall elected officials, for example? Are there ways to avoid dependence on a handful of leaders?

Re-imagining political parties and their relationships to social movements is an ongoing and urgent task, even if we acknowledge that it is full of contradictions. It is clear that really reimagining the role of parties requires reimagining institutions, to which I turn next.

4

Another State Is Possible

Project Cybersyn is today an odd historical footnote to the doomed socialist presidency of Salvador Allende in Chile, who was overthrown by US-backed military forces in 1973. Although it never came to full operational capacity, much of it was built: a network of telex machines connecting state enterprises and supercomputers receiving the latest economic data. At its center was an Operations Room that probably resembled the deck of *Star Trek*'s *Enterprise*: a number of high-tech Tulip chairs with advanced electronic controls arranged in a semicircle. Decision-makers occupying those seats would be able to make real-time decisions based on up-to-the-minute economic data fed by the network, while the supercomputer in the background would constantly run economic simulations. The whole system was designed so that decision-makers would be able to quickly absorb vast amounts of information and make speedy decisions, such as adjusting levels of input and output at state enterprises and utilities systems.

This was a high dream of socialist planning: a command economy made as flexible and nimble as its capitalist counterparts, thanks to technology and the latest scientific research. Today, of course, Cybersyn seems quaint and evokes an innocent time. Allende's overthrow had much less to do with economic inefficiencies than with the convergence of ambitions of capitalist elites, the military, and the US empire. But Cybersyn nonetheless represented a strain of thinking on the left that had found expression in socialist governments elsewhere: that institutions need to be centrally planned; and that there are correct policies that can be scientifically determined before being carried out.

To be fair to Cybersyn, we never got to see its potential fulfilled. The sudden overthrow of the Allende regime ended not only Cybersyn but also Allende's vision for a Chilean transition to socialism anchored in "people power." In its place, General Pinochet and his team of US-trained economic advisors installed a brutal model of free market capitalism combined with state repression. Out were socialist dreams, and in was a capitalist fantasy of the free market unfettered by democracy. It is to 1973, of course, that David Harvey and others date the international ascendancy of neoliberalism, the economic doctrine of untrammeled markets and minimal states.

Less well-known outside the region is the fact that at the time of the coup some urban planners under Allende had also been experimenting with different forms of participatory planning. They, and the thinking of the Santiago School, as it became known, then went on to influence leftist planners in neighboring countries in Latin America once they found themselves at the helm of local and regional governments in the 1980s and 1990s. Latin America became known in the 1990s as a continent full of participatory experiments, many drawing direct and indirect influence from those planners. Their ideas would echo throughout the continent: that state institutions are not monoliths, but could instead serve political and strategic purposes for the left; that planning—even under capitalism—could be a political instrument to socialist ends; and that local participatory politics could activate local publics into action and into bigger arenas. These and other ideas were circulating at the time and would provide a foundation for leftist experimentation with transforming institutions over the next decades.

Popular Participation: The Left's Hallmark

Even if it became a widespread and politically malleable idea in the 1990s, participatory governance emerged from the left sometime in the late 1970s and early 1980s. There is not just one founding example to point to. Whether it is the cooperative governance of Villa El Salvador in Peru or the participatory decision-making in Lages, Brazil, in the early 1980s is an academic question.

For some, participation was purely instrumental and part of an incremental strategy of socialist takeover of the bourgeois state in the longer term, a war of maneuver and occupation. But, for others, it was seen as a process of colonization and transformation of the state. But both perspectives bred genuine democratizing projects that emerged as authoritarian regimes were coming to an end.

As with political parties, the influence of liberation theology and popular education was central to this new participatory rethinking. Reforms were understood as a way to channel popular input to government actions and to democratize society itself in ways that movements by themselves could not. As political parties were being rethought as vehicles for social movement demands, so were state institutions, and participatory politics and reforms were seen as the way to do it.

Participatory Democracy, Brazilian Style

Over the course of the 1990s several cities in Brazil became internationally famous for their participatory reforms under the PT, like Belo Horizonte, Porto Alegre, Recife, and others. After early experimentation and failure in the early 1990s, PT administrators settled on a set of strategies that seemed to work and deliver electoral successes.

These reforms tended to be wide-ranging efforts that engaged high numbers of participants and gave them actual decision-making power. Often centered on (but not limited to) municipal budgets, reforms impacted a variety of areas of the local state. Their central feature was empowered decision-making at the neighborhood level. In some cities tens of thousands of mostly poor residents made important decisions on all manner of government affairs, sometimes deciding the whole city's budget for investment. Schools, health clinics, roads, and urban infrastructure were redistributed away from downtown areas toward peripheral ones in the name of a project of popular sovereignty.

Participatory budgeting has been among the best known of these efforts and is amply documented by researchers. In the hundreds of cities that implemented it, officials hosted meetings on a yearly cycle. These teach participants about the procedures, before drawing them into the process of proposing urban improvement projects. The cycle led to a final binding vote on government expenditures. In some cities as much as 10 percent of the adult population took part in this kind of budgeting.

It is important to note that instituting participatory democracy in this context went beyond just setting up meetings. Everywhere participation took place, there was a less visible but *crucially important set of institutional mechanisms* to give participatory democracy its teeth. To create an unbreakable link between popular will and government action—the goal of popular sovereignty in this context—meant minimizing veto points and discretionary changes by others. To have lots of decision-making meetings only in order to have decisions reversed or amended by experts or other officials would render the meetings meaningless. But to actually create the link required tangible changes, such as setting up municipal bureaucracies dedicated to overseeing the process and safeguarding its integrity. It meant creating offices of community relations within various departments. And finally there was a second-level "forum of forums" made up of participants to be the ultimate arbiter of the process in case of doubts or ambiguities.

Participation was understood as part of a transformative project, and as a tool to resolve the endemic problems of the leftists then in power. From the point of view of popular sovereignty, participation was based on *individual* (and not associational) representation. In other words, it was much less of a negotiation between collectives (say, municipal unions and housing movements) than a series of open mass meetings. This feature was democratizing in that it expanded the reach of participation beyond what social movements could achieve by themselves. It was also politically expedient in that it extended the legitimacy of the process beyond political allies. Individual participation, of course, also tipped the political balance away from movements, which explains why, in some settings, activists worried about too much state influence.

The political calculus was central. *Participatory reforms activated popular politics that could be a counterweight to elite interests.* Where participation worked, it allowed administrations to carry out pro-poor policies in a legitimate political framework. Applying transparent criteria, administrations were able to prioritize redistributive proposals, for example, reallocating the budget and setting up expenditures for poorer neighborhoods. In contrast to earlier leftist proposals in Latin America, participation moved the question of emancipation to institutions. In these spaces, we could glimpse political self-rule, effective popular control of the local state, and a local instantiation of popular sovereignty. Yet a question would arise, as some of these governments became quite successful at delivering "good governance": were they delivering good governance, or good governance from the left?

Making the Road by Walking: The Zapatistas

The Zapatista experiment in self-governance underway in the southern state of Chiapas since the 1990s provides an important counterpoint to some of the other Latin American examples when thinking about the possibilities for transforming institutions. Rather than transform existing institutions or add parallel institutions to existing ones, Zapatista strategy has revolved around creating new institutions in autonomous territories. Much is made of the separateness, particularly in English-language discussions that juxtapose it to "statism." But Zapatista emphasis on radical democracy and on reimagining how government could function under popular control makes it more like a logical extension of popular sovereignty than an exception. Zapatistas have gone further in this regard than many others in organizing structures under its guiding slogan of "*mandar obedeciendo* [leading by following]."

The EZLN (Ejército Zapatista de Liberación Nacional, the Zapatista Army of National Liberation), as the Zapatistas are formally known, was founded in 1983 in the Lacandona Forest in the southern Mexican state of Chiapas by activists linked to peasant organizations and other, earlier, organizations dedicated to armed struggle. It engaged in clandestine base-building activities, until 1 January 1994. On the day NAFTA came into effect, the EZLN made its first public declaration and began what would be a twelve-day war against the Mexican state. Demands included an end to neoliberalism in Mexico, the democratization of the Mexican state, popular control over natural resources and land in Chiapas, and indigenous rights. The insurgents gained control of some towns in the region before being overrun by the Mexican army. The cease-fire was followed by a treaty that granted some legal autonomy to indigenous regions. When the Mexican state violated that agreement in 1996, Zapatistas decided to begin forming their own governance structures in the region. Some 300,000 people today live in this territory, which includes over thirty municipalities and has a complete system of institutions of self-rule that include educational, health, justice, economic, and governance ones.

Governance is carried out by nonprofessional, volunteer, rotating, and bottom-up organizations always bound by the mandates of the community. Each of the municipalities is divided into communities (more than one thousand in total) that hold assemblies and elect participants into the higher tiers. Assemblies are the central element of Zapatista democracy, and function on a consensus basis. Participation of everyone over twelve is mandatory, and assemblies decide on most local matters. They also approve major governance decisions.

The most important institutions are above the municipality: five "Good Governance Councils" interspersed throughout the territory. These, run by a rotating group of twelve people, govern the region for a fixed term. They liaise with the outside world, for example, collectively purchasing goods if necessary, or managing the significant amount of volunteer donations that come in. There is an Information Committee that functions alongside each Good Governance Council, and a Vigilance Committee that is an independent watchdog on the Good Governance Councils. All major decisions of the Central Ruling Committee, the ultimate authority in the territory, must be approved by all assemblies. This ruling body is made up of elected pairs of men and women from each of the indigenous groups in the territory, along with one pair for the non-indigenous.

Other institutions in Zapatista territory are run similarly, such as its justice system or the system of trade between different territories. There is an overriding commitment to bottom-up democracy combined with a mix of indigenous practices (for example, principles of restoration in the justice system), a commitment to gender equality (such as set-asides on certain councils), pluralism (the various languages of instruction in the educational system), and practices that come from popular education and liberation theology.

Although Zapatistas are sometimes portrayed as

anarchists in English-language discussions and are juxtaposed to the more "statist" leftism of other Latin American countries, in Latin America the Zapatistas are usually understood on a continuum with other leftist movements and parties in the region, the choice of building alternate institutions in liberated territory more a result of its context than its ideology. Zapatista ideology, like the other examples in this book, emerges out of a flexible mix of Marxism, liberation theology, popular education, and indigenous concepts. The explicit commitment to participatory democracy, to democratizing both communities and institutions in search of a better world, puts them in explicit dialogue with other political projects in the region organized under popular sovereignty.

Zapatistas, too, have since the mid-2000s increasingly engaged other social movements and groups in ways that resemble the broad alliances on the left in Latin America. In 2006, the EZLN organized a trek from Zapatista territory to Mexico City. Called The Other Campaign (La Otra Campaña), the idea was to engage other movements on an egalitarian footing to build a movement to transform Mexico. The public statements leading up to The Other Campaign, from August 2005, are telling. Rather than seeking to be a vanguard of this movement, the EZLN understood that the movement needed a plural alliance of "workers, *campesinos*, students, workers in the city and the countryside" alongside indigenous people under a broad, anti-capitalist umbrella, creating "new forms of organization and new worlds." And in 2017 the Zapatistas publicly announced they would be supporting Maria de Jesús "Marichuy" Patricio, the National Indigenous Council's candidate for the presidency of Mexico, bringing their political targets back to the level of the national state.

Inside, Alongside, or Outside the System?

The examples of Zapatista experiments with institutions illustrate well some of the challenges of popular sovereignty. Both have been, in different ways, held up as models for participatory democracy to be emulated elsewhere. But too often the discussion is limited to only their most evident or surface features, such as neighborhood meetings or assemblies. To really draw political lessons from both means having to dig into the tougher questions of power and the dangers and potentials of institutionalization.

There are parallels with the issue of political

parties and representation. If "speaking for" representation implies a kind of closure that is inherent in political parties, institutions also imply closures. Institutions are made of routines, patterns, codifications, and legislation. And existing institutions reflect prior assumptions, decisions, and a social order. Whether we are speaking of municipal governments, an education department, or a ministry of planning, it does not matter if our allies win the election, these *institutions are not set up for popular sovereignty*. They are designed for managing populations, protecting the social order, and defending private property. When activists engage institutions they really do so in conditions not of their own choosing.

To build *separate* institutions in theory avoids the problem, allowing the popular imagination and democratic impulses to shape institutions according to another set of mandates altogether. But to do so means disengaging from the very institutions that are responsible for the inequalities that gave rise to our movements in the first place. Separation allows existing institutions to run unchecked and gives up important terrain. The theory of popular sovereignty recognizes this as one of the principal tensions when engaging institutions.

In Brazil, as in many other places, the idea was

to re-appropriate institutions by building participatory structures into them, thus rendering them
more porous and forcing them into transformation.
In Zapatista territory the idea was to build new
institutions altogether. In each case the idea has
been to expose institutions and institutional decisions to binding forms of popular will, by bringing
the people into institutions. And in each case, the
goal has been to both minimize the role of specific
experts and preset routines in favor of a maximal
expression of popular will and creativity.

In the Brazilian cases, the great danger is that
participation can be co-opted. Institutional patterns may be too deeply set, powerful interests may
be too entrenched, and participation may wind
up simply legitimating bureaucratic mandates and
political agendas set elsewhere. The "We" without
"sovereignty" is rhetorically powerful but politically nearly meaningless from the point of view of
popular sovereignty.

But the Zapatista solution has its own danger
as well: the potential for disengagement. Just as
co-optation is the risk of engaging existing institutions, disengagement is the danger of developing
separate institutions. It is worth remembering that
the Zapatistas chose for decades not to engage the
Mexican state, not because of an opposition to the

idea of a state as much as a strategic choice in a removed rural context and in the face of a "bad state." Of course, Zapatistas recognize this balancing act, as the occasional forays into other politics, such as endorsing a presidential candidate, imply.

How Participation Can Co-opt

Since the time of these first reforms in the 1990s, participation has caught on, and we have been living through a veritable "participation revolution" in Latin America and much of the Global North. The idea of introducing citizen participation into the political process has traceable origins in social movements and parties such as the Zapatistas and the PT. The cities of New York, Chicago, and London have introduced forms of participation that are directly due to these movements. Participation is, of course, usually very different in these places. It is not driven by social movement parties seeking social transformation, but rather by reformers within governments intent on bringing "citizens closer to government" and "ending apathy." There is very little focus on sovereignty, or decision-making over impactful decisions. There are more ways than ever to participate democratically today, but deciding is exercised over less and less.

Proponents will readily admit that these experiments, in and of themselves, are not meant to fundamentally challenge the structural inequalities rooted in capitalism or racism that are among principal threats to democracy today. But, the argument goes, they may serve as some kind of school of democracy, teaching people about how government works and building community power in the long term. Successful cases from Latin America are sometimes invoked as evidence.

A more skeptical view is in order: Latin American participatory reforms were much more thorough *and* were driven by a transformative political project, not "ending apathy." To stay with the "school of democracy" metaphor, we are speaking of quite different curricula. In terms of popular sovereignty, activists today facing the question of whether to engage instances of participation need to do serious questioning before mobilizing their communities and organizations. Whether we are speaking of a public consultation on zoning or a participatory process to decide on social service projects, activists need to determine how much emphasis there is on *empowered decision-making over significant decisions* and how much room there is for participants to determine the terms of participation itself. This needs to be assessed in each context.

Many of these experiments today take place at the margins of the state apparatus, without significant government reform and without transforming the functioning of state institutions. They often invoke the language of empowerment without significant decision-making by participants. Many are introduced from above and do not allow for participants to define the terms. Many of these experiments do not create links to governmental authority, and the ones that do stay away from decisions that matter most to the community, such as economic policies, zoning, or policing.

A concern is that participation, and the time and effort it involves, can become detached from issues that are crucial to communities. This could imply re-routing community effort and organizing away from issues that are pressing from the point of view of social justice. Social movements have limited capacity, and it is worrisome for it to be spent on agendas dictated by administrative possibilities rather than more autonomous conversations about needs. Participation in this way becomes a technical solution, rather than a political method of emancipation. The kind of participation that is encouraged is non-conflictual, collaborative, and emphasizes self-regulation and community problem-solving within limited terms of what is possible. Never in play are the kinds of seemingly impossible demands and courageous tactics that have always made social change.

Another very real concern is that participation is very effective at generating legitimacy for the status quo. There are endless forums today asking participants to decide on limited choices—such as where to cut back social spending (as opposed to whether spending should be cut back at all), or on the kinds of amenities at a newly up-zoned luxury neighborhood (as opposed to whether the neighborhood should have been up-zoned at all). A high degree of discretion over participation's outcomes remains in the hands of others, and it is very easy to turn it into a mechanism to simply legitimate political authority and tamp down conflict.

Especially worrisome in this climate of retrenchment is the concern that participation can move energies away from associational or sectoral representation. It is not uncommon for promoters of participation today to frame their appeals as a way of going "beyond" unions, social movements, neighborhood associations, interest groups, and placing emphasis on "regular citizens." Collectives are given no role. But this emphasis on direct voice can come into conflict with and disempower associations, movements, and unions as the necessary counterweights to status quo injustices.

Transforming Institutions

One of the most vexing problems facing activists today is how to relate to formal state institutions. Much of the hesitation emerges from an inability to imagine the state beyond its negative and repressive functions, or to imagine a kind of decision-making compatible with radically democratic impulses. As I discussed earlier, popular sovereignty invites us to rethink all state institutions, as it reframes what it means for the people to exert power over them. It means asking two questions: Does the institution reflect the radically democratic will, and does it serve to further democratize society?

In the case of Latin American experiences, institutions were reformed (or built anew alongside existing institutions) so that they might reach in the direction of popular sovereignty. Several lessons remain. First is that these were *democratizing* reforms of the state. Institutions were reoriented to serve a democratized will, and to serve a democratizing role in the context of sovereign decision-making.

Participation was a hallmark of these reforms: *never for its own sake*, but as a way to bring the people into the state to *exercise control over it* and to make sure it served a democratizing function in society. This fundamentally implied reframing the role of expertise and experts who had to serve the democratic will, and not the other way around.

These reforms were part of a political project. Since it was understood at the time that the state is not a monolith, these experiments took place at scales and settings more likely to be porous, like a municipal government, or at a regional education department. But the ease of reform of a particular institution was never a driving factor in itself—participation was instituted over matters of important pre-existing concern. Democratizing these institutions was always part of a strategy of reforms that would eventually include other levels of government and the national state. This is as true of municipal reforms in Brazil as in the development of alternate institutions in Zapatista territory. The Zapatistas will not have sovereign control over their own lives until significant reforms happen at the level of the national Mexican state, at the level of ownership of production, and at the level of the world economy. This was always clearly recognized, as was the fact that reforms were to be ongoing, always open to new popular imaginations of how they should be arranged.

These institutional reforms were also understood as a way to incubate radical popular politics. Participation in these institutions was thought to have the ability to encourage activism, broaden activists' horizons, and empower them to contest expert mandates. These were very much understood as places to learn—but explicitly within the context of a broader political project of social transformation. The writings of the era show a clear and constant concern with the possibility of co-optation and bureaucratization of movements. There was a lot of worry about replacing movement horizons (such as liberation, utopia, internationalism) with governmental horizons (deadlines, yearly cycles, governance).

It is against this backdrop that the choices of inside/alongside/outside strategies for institutions were made, often reflecting particular political contexts rather than prior ideological commitments, and usually fully aware of the limits of a particular strategic choice. If an exclusively inside strategy has the danger of co-optation, a strictly outside one has the danger of disengagement and withdrawal from key arenas.

In the end, the theory and lessons of popular

sovereignty in Latin American give us more of a broad orientation for engaging state institutions than specific recipes for doing so. In the context of today's enthusiasm for participation, thinking about sovereignty, self-determination, and broader political projects is an important rejoinder to investing movement energies in tokenistic participation over trivial matters, or giving legitimacy to forums that come with pre-set agendas. At the same time, both the PT and Zapatista stories are remarkable examples of what unleashing the imagination on the question of institutions as part of a transformative political project can accomplish.

Conclusion

Twenty-First Century Popular Sovereignty

Popular sovereignty, in its radical variant, is both a theory of democracy and a transformative political project. As a theory of democracy, it asks questions of our institutions in a completely different way than liberal democracy might. Rather than beginning (and ending) by asking the formal rules of democracy (are there "free" elections?), its questions are always substantive: who makes up the people, and do the people rule? And as a transformative political project, it calls for a reinvention of democracy that places the oppressed at the center of an ever-renewing "we" that is fundamentally empowered to decide concerning the conditions of its collective life. The political community at its center is open, egalitarian, and plural, and it insists on always asking if it is operating democratically. And the question of its rule, the people's rule, is similarly always questioned: is it real, and is it operating democratically?

We need to place that transformative political project at the center of any discussion of engaging with institutions in the twenty-first century. To return to the questions that motivated the introduction to this book: what is urgently needed now is careful and strategic thinking about sites for institutional engagement, leveraging some of the lessons from a previous generation of activists who achieved a lot in very difficult circumstances. This task is meaningful today, in the context of an increasingly globalized world, and when the stakes for people's livelihoods are higher than ever before. We need to think about winning smaller battles as well as accumulating victories in a context in which right-wing interests are organized, and too often winning. Today's is a context in which the project of political construction of a people is being lost to radically conservative forces that have no qualms in fully engaging in that contest. This also means, among other things, facing the limit situations of popular sovereignty, and understanding why undertaking such a project requires thinking beyond the nation-state and private property.

Conclusion

Pink Tide: Inclusion and Transformation

Before turning to some of the specific lessons from the preceding chapters, it is important to consider what the Pink Tide was and what it was not. The Pink Tide has been a remarkable chapter in the history of Latin America, one with very important lessons for the left everywhere. The widely documented material gains alone for poor and working-class people were remarkable, pulling tens of millions of people out of poverty, reducing inequality, and granting, often for the first time in parts of the region, widespread access to education, healthcare, and food. Across left-of-center governments there was increased public-sector spending on education, health, infrastructure, and cash-transfer programs to the poor. There were real increases in the minimum wage, stark reductions in poverty, and reduced inequality rates—reversing patterns of the 1980s and 1990s. There has been upward mobility for working-class and poor people, and in some places there it is now possible to speak of indigenous and black middle classes in a way that wasn't possible before. While it is important to critically assess this legacy, it is important that these gains always stand in the background, reminding us what this moment has meant for the continent's poor.

These governments also pushed back against US hegemony in the region, effectively reversing decades of influence for the first time. The proposed Free Trade of the Americas Agreement was famously undone by Pink Tide governments in the mid-2000s, but just as important were quieter victories, such as preventing US initiatives to extend the War on Terror to the continent. And some policies—such as Bolivia's renationalization of its hydrocarbons, would have been unthinkable in the absence of a tide of national regimes willing to stand up to Washington.

And across countries—these starkly unequal, racist, violent, *machista*, and often conservative societies—there was an introduction of a broad and generative conception of social justice to both policies and mainstream discussions. These ranged from indigenous self-determination in Bolívia and the rights of Afro-descendants and affirmative action policies in Brazil, to advances of LGBT rights in Argentina and Uruguay, the discussions of the rights of nature in the Ecuadorian constitution, and the discussions of gender parity in Chilean political institutions. While the activists behind such projects would be the first to admit these are all entirely incomplete, every one of these also represents a previously unthinkable horizon in their respective societies.

Conclusion

And this, in the end, is the legacy the Pink Tide represents. Throughout the region these movements scored remarkable concrete victories, locally, regionally, sectorally, managing to craft fluid intersectional and socialist coalitions that managed at times to connect to social justice, human rights, feminism, LGBT issues, and environmental issues in ways that would have seemed unthinkable just a few years before. All-consuming theoretical debates (reform or revolution? class or identity?) were for a time relegated to the background where they belong. In their place arose concrete questions about creating "another world" in the here and now, as the slogan went. And in places they were able to catch a glimpse of that world, whether in a rural cooperative on collectively owned land with production along socialist principles, a local government supporting the struggles of trans sex workers, or in the running of a local school that introduced indigenous language and history for the first time. And in doing so, they pushed political horizons to new frontiers. There is no way to undo these victories or erase them from popular memory, whatever one's ultimate analysis of the political parties and governments that rose and fell. When the political pendulum swings back, as it will, it will build as much on the lessons taken from the failures as on the successes. We need to also reflect on these lessons while moving away from armchair "inevitablism" that concludes that these were doomed projects from the start.

The lessons are political ones.

PT founder Olívio Dutra has used a phrase to describe the PT national government that captures its limits well: it was a government of inclusion but not of transformation. Millions of people were included for the first time, and many of them were recognized and heard. But many structures in Brazil were not changed—not the political system, not land tenure, not the tax system, not media ownership, not urban systems, and not elite influence on the judiciary. And it was over those grounds that many important battles were lost. The party's hesitation to undertake political reform may have been one of its undoings. Many within the party had long proposed reforms to transform the country's broken political system and weaken the power of elites and oligarchs and their corrupt politicians. This would have included limiting the private funding of political elections and donations, introducing mechanisms of transparency and accountability, and creating stricter rules for the formation of political parties. In the end, even if the logic was one of necessity, too many politicians elected through the PT wound up taken in by status-quo political modes of operation. Media reform may have been another set of missed transformations, as the battle for hearts and minds over the airwaves in Brazil became an all-out scorched-earth assault by its monopolistic media in the months and weeks before the legislative coup.

The party's difficulty in getting to transformation speaks to both the organized and entrenched power of elites as well as to the ways that the structures of the state work to their advantage and why they offer so much resistance to their reforms. The examples in this book—from Allende's overthrow to right-wing revanchism in Brazil—could be joined by many others in Latin America that show the resistance of organized capitalist interests to popular sovereignty. Foreign interference is common in many of these instances, and many activists are only now coming to appreciate how this takes the form not only of battleships stationed offshore but also of consultants in the art of toppling leftist regimes. Sometimes this comes as a frontal assault, and sometimes, as in the case of Brazil, this is predated by years of partial accommodation, quiet organizing, and holding of positions within key institutions. In retrospect, the opponents of popular sovereignty seldom respected the rules of the democratic contest.

But in the end, it was also the party's inability to remain true to its radical democratic roots that accounts for the character of its national tenure. This included the hardening of its leadership structure, the closing off of decision-making to party leaders, the emphasis on electors as opposed to militants, the lack of empowered national participatory democracy, and its preference for coalition and compromises in Parliament over the activation of popular politics. The activation of popular politics as a counterweight to organized elite interests through participatory reforms had been an absolutely central element of the party's earlier successes at local levels.

Popular Sovereignty and the Global North: The United States?

In retrospect the Latin American context of the 1980s finds some similarities in the US of today. This is seen in sharply increasing inequalities, lack of credible institutional outlets, uncertainty about rights and freedoms, a precarious and splintered job market, the hollowing of public provision—alongside radical resistance and real hope in local arenas. It is not surprising that questions facing movements today—whether and how to engage political parties and institutions, whether to be part of a system that was not made for us—find echoes in the history of Latin American movements and parties of the 1990s and onwards. The more pointed concern of whether to participate in a system premised on racial subjugation is also shared. This has been a debate among indigenous activists at the formation of the both the MAS and the EZLN, just as it is has been present in Black radical thought in the US at least since Reconstruction. The powerful idea of Abolition Democracy, as originally articulated by W.E.B. Dubois, of abolishing institutions of subjugation as part of a transformative political project from below, finds deep resonance with these debates about popular sovereignty as well.

It is important not to forget that radical energies exist and continue to bubble up in many places, including in the United States. In addition to the movements already mentioned, nobody will forget the courageous #NODAPL struggle at Standing Rock that from 2016 pitted the principles of indigenous sovereignty and environmental stewardship against profiteering, manifest destiny, and the militarized state. The near-daily protests since early 2017 against the Trump administration and its policies have also been remarkable in their rainbow of coalitions and efforts, such as #ItTakesRoots #ToGrowTheResistance, a radically democratic multiracial coalition fighting for racial, housing, and climate justice to build "visionary opposition" to the regime.

And beyond those, there are many ongoing local efforts that take place mostly away from headlines. Movements led by working-class people of color around issues of livelihood, for example, have flourished in these hard times. This would include the work of Critical Resistance, which fights for prison abolition through chapters throughout the country. It would also include the movement for utility justice in upstate New York led by Nobody Leaves Mid-Hudson and Causa Justa's Oakland-based building-by-building organizing work against displacement and gentrification in California. Also participating in these struggles is New York City's ALIGN, a labor and community coalition that fights for environmental and economic justice and racial equity. And Homes For All is a national movement that unites the struggles of dozens of these efforts.

US labor, too, shows signs, often below the surface, of a radicalism that may not always be apparent at the level of national leadership. These include activists who have successfully radical-ized shop-floor struggles to extend them to other injustices, who have fought to democratize union structures, and who have taken broad social movement and social justice concerns as their own—not as afterthought. One powerful example among very many is the Chicago Teachers Union, which partners with community and racial justice groups to work on issues such as the school-to-prison pipeline.

And there are examples of building local power from below. One is exemplified by Make The Road New York, which tackles economic and social justice issues while investing in immigrant leadership. And among the most inspiring is Cooperation Jackson, in Mississipi, which has built on the tradition of cooperatives and worker-owned enterprises to fight for economic justice, self-determination, and democratic rights for the black community.

Between all of these and others, it is clear that we, in the United States, do not lack for foundations of a radically democratic new, leftist, transformative political project that draws on popular creativity and imagination. It also clear that in actual, concrete struggles, as in the above, sterile academic ideological debate is much less important than strategic discussion anchored in the arts of solidarity.

Across the Global North the urgent task before us is articulating multi-racial, multi-community, and multi-class coalitions for transformative social change while finding ways to translate and connect the energies of our social movements with institutional engagements and transformations in ways that do not turn those into instruments of legitimation for a broken political system. The center and moral compass of that popular bloc needs to be occupied by *oppressed communities* and their ambition to achieve social transformation.

But what we do not yet have is a structure of political representation—whether it takes the form or name of a party or not—that amplifies and connects these struggles, that has an institutional face, that leads by following, and that helps bring about a broader vision while enabling specific struggles, helping paint the "concrete fantasy" that inspires our collective voices. It will have to balance the choices Latin Americans faced—recognizing and privileging individuals or groups, formalizing or not, finding ways to remain democratic—as well as others they did not, such as how to face the urgency of climate change. During this development of a structure of political representation we will need to absolutely rethink what it means to engage institutions, abolishing, transforming, and re-inventing them in ways that give expression to our creativity, that empower communities to decide on matters that affect them, that balance inside and outside strategies, and that activate the popular politics that enable these transformations.

Popular Sovereignty Beyond Private Property and The Nation State

Popular sovereignty as a political project is open-ended as to its ultimate destination, and even then, it provides more of a methodology than a road-map. Its insistence on popular agency and capacity discourages too much abstract utopian thinking disconnected from concrete struggles and histories, which is why I have insisted on exploring it as I have in the preceding pages. It has had a lot of appeal on the left, and the coalitions I have described in these pages have been socialist and anti-capitalist ones, inspired by plural utopias, but that all looked to a world beyond classes and private property and beyond the bourgeois nation-state. For this reason I close this manuscript with some very brief gestures aimed at describing popular sovereignty's end-game, specifically what it might look like beyond locales or nations.

As a theory of democracy, and quite unlike liberal democracy, popular sovereignty is bound neither to nation-states nor to the sanctity of private property. In fact, a radically open, expanding, and egalitarian conception of the people pushes against the boundaries of nation-states, just as true popular sovereignty is limited by private property. A couple of examples, among many possible ones: indigenous nations that extend beyond the borders of nation-states; or transnational networks of peasant farmers such as Via Campesina, which conceives of a people with no respect at all for boundaries. And it is not hard to think of many examples like the ones I have described in this book, which have pitted popular sovereignty against private property. The very term "private property" implies something beyond the reach of the people.

If we follow this line of thinking to its logical conclusions, autonomy, being *autonomos*, having self-rule, cannot then be defined as separateness but rather as something like linked interdependence. There are many instances where it is impossible to self-rule without reference to extra-local settings. An island-state becoming submerged owing to sea-level rise, for example, is not able to locally decide not to sink without reference to regulating emissions that are produced elsewhere, enabling energy consumption at yet a third place. Self-rule in this conception means that all autonomies are interconnected. How to concretely connect all of these interdependent autonomies without falling back into the nation-state form—or how to begin that in concrete terms by engaging and transforming existing institutions—is a question I can't answer in this space, but there has been much thinking on this question from the time of the World Social Forum onwards, within movements such as Via Campesina or the recent *acampadas* in Europe.

This is important to signal because one of the criticisms of popular sovereignty proposals is that they seem too local when we have so many pressing global issues, such as climate change. What can Cooperation Jackson, or a teachers' union, or Bolivian social movements, or any of the other examples here have to do with such global topics? Yet it is the expansive conception of democracy in operation in those places that has something vitally important to contribute. We need to radically expand the reach of the demos, not only because it is normatively desirable but because it is necessary. The lack of more decisive action on environmental regulation to date owes more to power asymmetries and the outsized influence of private interests than it does to coordination problems between nations or "ignorant publics." Entirely off the table at consultations and summits on climate change, for example, are solutions that hinge on the kinds of radical solidarity or power over private property that we see in places where popular sovereignty is manifest.

Whether we are speaking of the specifics of global trade policy, global property rights to water, environmental regulation, or the management of complex financial instruments, there are an increasing number of important decisions that take place in settings completely beyond the reach of the demos, where powerful interests can most fully express themselves without sanction. A robust and transformative conception of democracy, like the one I have laid out here, not only insists on popular power over such decisions but is also unfettered by the idea of the nation-state or the sanctity of private property. Even if we have not figured out the precise institutional arrangements to enact popular sovereignty globally does not mean we should dismiss its relevance as a framework. The road, as the saying goes, will be made by walking it.

Further Reading

Akuno, Kali, and Ajamu Nangwaya, eds. *Jackson Rising: The Struggle for Economic Democracy and Black Self-Determination in Jackson, Mississippi*. Montreal: Daraja Press, 2017.

Anria, Santiago. Social Movements, Party Organization, and Populism: Insights from the Bolivian MAS. *Latin American Politics and Society* 55.3 (2013): 19–46.

Aronowitz, Stanley. *The Death and Life of American Labor: Toward a New Workers' Movement*. London: Verso, 2014.

Ciccariello-Maher, George. *Building the Commune: Radical Democracy in Venezuela*. London: Verso, 2016.

Colloredo-Mansfeld, Rudi. *Fighting like a Community: Andean Civil Society in an Era of Indian Uprisings*. University of Chicago Press, 2009.

Dangl, Benjamin. *Dancing with Dynamite: Social Movements and States in Latin America*. Oakland: AK Press, 2010.

Davis, Angela Y. *Abolition Democracy: Beyond Empire, Prisons, and Torture*. New York: Seven Stories Press, 2011.

Della, Porta D., Joseba Fernández, Hara Kouki, and Lorenzo Mosca. *Movement Parties against Austerity*. Cambridge, UK: Polity, 2017.

Further Reading

Dixon, Chris. *Another Politics: Talking Across Today's Transformative Movements*. Berkeley: University of California Press, 2014.

Dussel, Enrique. *Twenty Theses on Politics*. Durham, NC: Duke University Press, 2008.

Errejón, Íñigo, and Chantal Mouffe. *Podemos: In the Name of the People*. London: Lawrence & Wishart, 2016.

Freire, Paulo. *The Pedagogy of the Oppressed*. New York: Bloomsbury, 2015.

Gould-Wartofsky, Michael A. *The Occupiers: The Making of the 99 Percent Movement*. New York: Oxford University Press, 2015.

Gutierrez, Gustavo. *A Theology of Liberation: History, Politics, and Salvation*, 15th anniversary ed., trans. Caridad Inda and John Eagleson. Maryknoll: Orbis, 1988.

Harnecker, Marta. *Rebuilding the Left*. London: Zed Books, 2007.

Hunter, Wendy. *The Transformation of the Workers' Party in Brazil, 1989–2009*. Cambridge, UK, and New York: Cambridge University Press, 2010.

Keck, Margaret E. *The Workers' Party and Democratization in Brazil*. New Haven: Yale University Press 1995.

Khan-Cullors, Patrisse, and Asha Bandele. *When They Call You a Terrorist: A Black Lives Matter Memoir*. New York: St. Martins, 2018.

Klein, Hillary. *Compañeras: Zapatista Women's Stories*. New York: Seven Stories Press, 2015.

Losier, Toussaint. Prison Movement History for the Era of #BlackLivesMatter. *Social Justice* 43.3 (2016): 112.

Loureiro P. M. Reformism, Class Conciliation and the Pink Tide: Material Gains and Their Limits. In M. Ystanes and I. Strønen (eds.), *The Social Life of Economic Inequalities in Contemporary Latin America: Approaches to Social Inequality and Difference*. London: Palgrave Macmillan, 2018.

Postero, Nancy G. *The Indigenous State: Race, Politics, and*

Further Reading

Performance in Plurinational Bolivia. Berkeley: University of California Press, 2017.

Rice, Roberta. From the Ground Up: The Challenge of Indigenous Party Consolidation in Latin America." *Party Politics* 17.2 (2011): 171–88.

Riofrancos, Thea. Democracy without the People. *N+1* 6.2 (2017).

Sitrin, Marina A., and Dario Azzellini. *They Can't Represent Us!: Reinventing Democracy from Greece to Occupy*. London: Verso, 2014.

Stahler-Sholk, Richard, H. Vanden, and M. Becker, eds. *Rethinking Latin American Social Movements: Radical Action from Below*. Lanham: Rowman & Littlefield, 2014.

Vergara-Camus, Leandro. *Land and Freedom: The MST, the Zapatistas and Peasant Alternatives to Neoliberalism*. London: Zed Books, 2014.

Weber, Jeffrey. *Red October: Left-Indigenous Struggles in Modern Bolivia*. Chicago: Haymarket Books, 2012.

Young, Kevin. *Blood of the Earth: Resource Nationalism, Revolution, and Empire in Bolivia*. Austin: University of Texas Press, 2017.

Zibechi, Raúl. *Dispersing Power: Social Movements as Anti-State Forces*. Oakland, CA: AK Press, 2010.